MAKING SENSE OF **HISTORY**
1509–1745

JOHN D. CLARE
ALEC FISHER
RICHARD KENNETT

DYNAMIC LEARNING

HODDER EDUCATION
AN HACHETTE UK COMPANY

The Schools History Project

Set up in 1972 to bring new life to history for students aged 13–16, the Schools History Project continues to play an innovatory role in secondary history education. From the start, SHP aimed to show how good history has an important contribution to make to the education of a young person. It does this by creating courses and materials which both respect the importance of up-to-date, well-researched history and provide enjoyable learning experiences for students.

Since 1978 the Project has been based at Trinity and All Saints University College Leeds. It continues to support, inspire and challenge teachers through the annual conference, regional courses and website: http://www.schoolshistoryproject.org.uk. The Project is also closely involved with government bodies and awarding bodies in the planning of courses for Key Stage 3, GCSE and A level.

Although every effort has been made to ensure that website addresses are correct at time of going to press, Hodder Education cannot be held responsible for the content of any website mentioned in this book. It is sometimes possible to find a relocated web page by typing in the address of the home page for a website in the URL window of your browser.

Hachette UK's policy is to use papers that are natural, renewable and recyclable products and made from wood grown in sustainable forests. The logging and manufacturing processes are expected to conform to the environmental regulations of the country of origin.

Orders: please contact Bookpoint Ltd, 130 Milton Park, Abingdon, Oxon OX14 4SE. Telephone: +44 (0)1235 827720. Fax: +44 (0)1235 400454. Lines are open 9.00a.m.–5.00p.m., Monday to Saturday, with a 24-hour message answering service. Visit our website at www.hoddereducation.co.uk

© John D. Clare, Alec Fisher, Richard Kennett

First published in 2014 by

Hodder Education,

An Hachette UK company

Carmelite House

50 Victoria Embankment

London EC4Y 0DZ

Impression number 10 9 8 7 6 5 4 3 2

Year 2018 2017 2016

Cover photo © Holmes Garden Photos/Alamy

Illustrations by Barking Dog Art, Peter Lubach, Tony Randell and Sebastian Quigley

Design layouts by Lorraine Inglis Design

Typeset in PMN Caecilia Light 10/13pt

Printed in Italy

A catalogue record for this title is available from the British Library

ISBN 978 14718 07879

The Publishers would like to thank the following for permission to reproduce copyright material:

Photo credits

Text acknowledgements

Contents

Investigating the Early Modern Era

The execution of Charles I

When the author team started writing this textbook, we were asked to choose ONE event, which for us would 'define the age' – the event which says most about what the period was like … which best gives us 'a sense of the period'.

When we wrote the first book in the series on the Middle Ages we selected the death of Thomas Becket (1170). For this book, we have chosen the execution of Charles I in 1649. The choice tells you a lot about us as historians and – at the end of this book – you will get your chance to disagree!

To be fair to us, nobody would suggest that the execution of Charles I was not a very important event.

It certainly created a stir when it happened. There was an agonised groan from the huge crowd. People rushed forward to dip their handkerchiefs in the blood; within ten days a book – the *Eikon Baslike* – declared Charles a religious martyr.

So this was, clearly, a very significant moment in British history … but does it 'define the age'?

Pages 2–3 will give you the chance to consider what it tells us about those times.

The execution of Charles I – the facts

On Tuesday, 30 January 1649 – after seven years of civil war – King Charles I was brought to the Banqueting Hall at Whitehall for execution. The scaffold was packed with officers and clergy, and protected by soldiers from the huge crowd.

The block was only 25cm high, so the king had to lie down to place his head on it. Then the masked executioner chopped off his head.

Activity

1 Work in a group of two or three. Study picture A. Make a list of TEN things you can see in the picture.
2 For each of the ten things, discuss what it suggests about life in these times, especially:
   ▌ politics (such as who ruled, how they ruled, the power of the army, the role of ordinary people)
   ▌ society (such as wealth, attitudes, behaviour, social class, the role of women, fashion, transport, buildings)
   ▌ beliefs (such as religion and superstitions).
3 Discuss as a whole class: 'What does picture A tell us about the period 1509–1745?' (Remember, you are inferring from an engraving, copied by someone who was biased and not there at the time. How reliable do you think your conclusions are?)

The first engraving of Charles' execution was published in Amsterdam (where the artist would be safe from arrest). The artist has got basic details wrong – the block was only 25cm high and the Banqueting Hall had two storeys. Some elements of the engraving are more symbolic than realistic – for instance, many paintings of the crucifixion show the Virgin Mary fainting (compare the woman at the bottom right).

This engraving, moreover, is not the Dutch original, but a rough German copy of it. In copying the original, the engraver has managed to 'flip' the image, so that it is back to front. He has also added significant details – divine clouds over the Banqueting Hall, with sunbeams pouring down onto the scene, and an angel giving the king a crown as he ascends into heaven. This artist clearly supported King Charles!

⬆ *The Beheading of King Charles I*

Welcome to the Early Modern Era!

When you studied 'The Middle Ages', you learned it was a term invented by the people of the Renaissance to condemn the period 400–1500AD as a time of decline and stupidity in between their own times and the times of the Ancient Greeks and Romans.

Although you learned that 'the Middle Ages' were far from being either slow or stupid, there is no doubt that the period which followed them was a time of rapid and exciting change.

The years 1509–1745 were a time when people fought and killed each other over religion. These were the years when Columbus discovered the 'New World' (1492), and when the English executed their king (1649).

They were years of rapid price inflation which affected both kings and peasants. They were years when England underwent a 'commercial revolution', built an empire, and became a 'top nation'.

Many historians have felt that you can see in these years the beginnings of our modern world, and for that reason they have called the period 'the Early Modern Era'.

Activity

▌ Where on the timeline would you place:
▌ the Norman Conquest
▌ the reign of Henry VIII
▌ the First World War?

1st	2nd	3rd	4th	5th	6th	7th	8th	9th	10th
1–99			300–99					800–99	

|———— ROMAN BRITAIN ————| |———————— SAXON AND VIKING ENGLAND ————————|
THE EARLY MIDDLE AGES

The numbering of years begins from the birth of Jesus Christ. BC means Before Christ. AD means Anno Domini 'In the year of our Lord (Jesus Christ)'.

Renaissance
A time of discovery and learning – and of wonderful buildings and paintings – as people tried to copy the Greeks and the Romans.

'The New World'
Christopher Columbus discovered the West Indies in 1492. Britain built an empire in North America in the eighteenth century.

Reformation
A period of violent change in religion, especially in northern Europe, when 'Protestant' Christians rejected the Roman Catholic Church.

Does the timeline show all of British history?

No! People have been living in Britain for many centuries. Before the Romans, Britain was dominated by a vibrant and violent Celtic 'Iron Age' culture of huge fortified hill forts and mystical, abstract artwork. How many people would you need to add to the left-hand side of the timeline to go back to the Uffington White Horse (1000BC)?

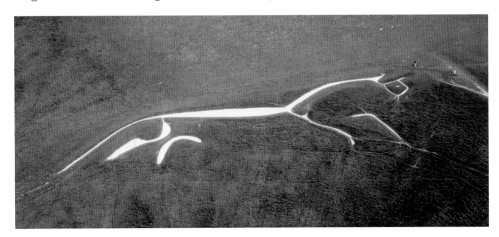

← The Uffington White Horse in Oxfordshire may be as old as 1000BC. It was made by stripping the thin grass turf from the white chalk rock beneath. There were many such horses made in Britain before the Romans arrived. Nobody knows why they were made, but archaeologists believe they may have had a religious purpose.

YOU

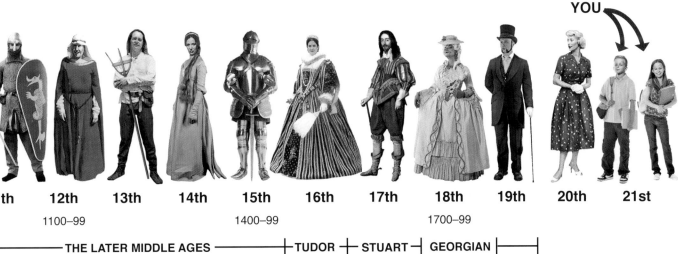

| th | 12th | 13th | 14th | 15th | 16th | 17th | 18th | 19th | 20th | 21st |

1100–99   1400–99   1700–99

———— THE LATER MIDDLE AGES ————┤ TUDOR ┼ STUART ┤ GEORGIAN ├
ENGLAND   BRITAIN   BRITAIN
├─ THE EARLY MODERN ERA ─┤   VICTORIAN
BRITAIN

THE RENAISSANCE   THE ENLIGHTENMENT

THE DISCOVERY AND COLONISATION OF THE 'NEW WORLD'

THE REFORMATION

THE COMMERCIAL REVOLUTION

├──── THE 'LITTLE ICE AGE' ────┤

Commercial Revolution
In the seventeenth century, the Dutch, French and English established worldwide bases, trading networks and empires.

The Little Ice Age
A long period of freezing winters and wet summers, which regularly ruined harvests and caused famines.

Enlightenment
Characterised by a desire for factual knowledge, science and political ideas such as liberty, **fraternity** and equality.

What about the weather?

The Early Modern Era was very different to the Middle Ages, not least in its weather, as you can see from the graph below!

A

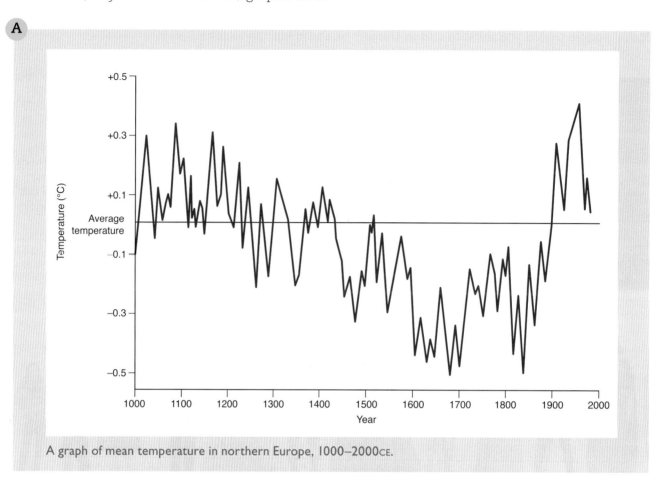

A graph of mean temperature in northern Europe, 1000–2000CE.

Activity

2 Working in a small group, discuss graph A and what it shows.
Draw a rough copy of the graph and mark onto it the following labels:
▌ Medieval Warm Period
▌ Little Ice Age
▌ Early Modern Era, 1509–1745.

3 Working in your group, then sharing as a whole class, make a list of the possible effects a large fall in temperatures might have had:
▌ for farming and the production of food
▌ for the economy (trade, travel and industry etc.).

4 Some years, temperatures fell so low that the River Thames froze over, and a fair was held on the ice. Study picture B. If the author team had decided that this picture of an ice fair in 1683 (not the one of Charles's execution on page 3) 'defined the age', what would you have inferred about the Early Modern Era? Discuss this as a whole class.

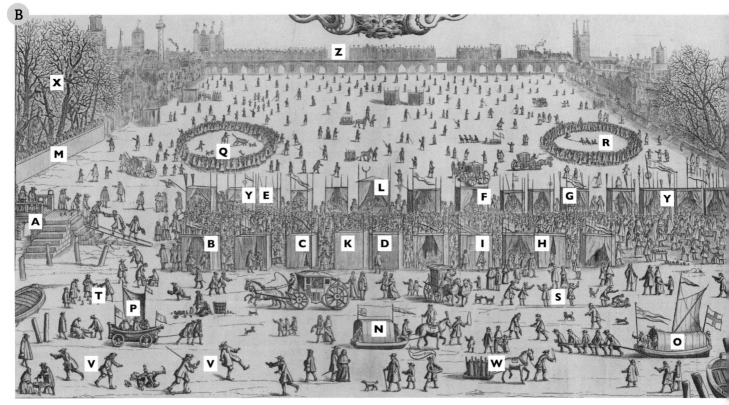

An etching sold in 1684 by the London printer William Warter, entitled: *AN Exact and lively REPRESENTATION of Booths and all the varieties of shows upon the ICE on the River of THAMES by LONDON in 1683*. The letters represent the following things:

A	The Temple Stairs with people going upon the ice to Temple Street.	**N**	The boat drawn by a horse.
B	The Duke of York's coffee house.	**O**	The Drum Boat.
C	The Tory Booth.	**P**	The boat drawn upon wheels.
D	The booth with a Phoenix on it.	**Q**	The bull baiting.
E	The Roast Beef Booth.	**R**	The chair sliding in the ring.
F	The halfway house.	**S**	The boys sliding.
G	The Bear garden Shire Booth.	**T**	The nine pin playing.
H	The Music Booth.	**V**	The sliding on skates.
I	The Printing Booth.	**W**	The sledge drawing coals from the other side of the Thames.
K	The Lottery Booth.	**X**	The boys climbing upon the tree in the Temple garden to see the bull baiting.
L	The Horn Tavern Booth.	**Y**	The toy shops.
M	The Temple garden with crowds of people looking over the wall.	**Z**	London Bridge.

Meet the people of the Early Modern Era

The people of the Middle Ages were divided into three groups – the fighters (the king, nobles and knights), the people who prayed (priests and monks) and the people who worked (villeins and craftsmen).

But things had changed by the Early Modern Era. The Wars of the Roses (1455–85) had ruined many of the nobility. After 1485, the ministers of the Tudor kings and queens increasingly came from a new 'middle class' of lawyers and **gentry**. Also, the scarcity of labourers after the **Black Death** (1348–50) forced many lords to free their **villeins**. After 1574 every Englishman was by law a 'freeman'.

When the **statistician** Gregory King came to write his *Observations and Conclusions upon the State and Condition of England* in 1696, therefore, he described society very differently. He divided English society into 'ranks and degrees':

High titles and skills – 63,000 families

This rank included the **aristocracy**, knights and lords of the manor, posh London gentlemen, scholars and men of letters, the clergy and government officers. Those with 'high titles and skills' were, in many respects, above the law.

Commerce – 50,000 families

This category included traders of all ranks, from the richest merchants to small tradesmen and shopkeepers. England's trade increased steadily after the middle of the seventeenth century, causing the **economist** Adam Smith to describe England in 1776 as 'a nation of shopkeepers'.

Industry – 60,000 families

The **Industrial Revolution** did not happen until the eighteenth century, but textiles and mining were steadily becoming more important in the economy throughout the period.

Were lords above the law?

In 1667 an army clerk named Carr petitioned the House of Commons that his commanding officer, Lord Gerard, had tried to bully Carr into giving him £2000 extra in his salary, and had beaten up Carr's wife when he refused to hand over the money. Hearing of the case, the House of Lords fined Carr £1000, put him in the stocks, imprisoned him, and burned his petition in public!

The poor – 794,000 families

In this category, King included 364,000 families of labourers and servants, 400,000 families of **cottagers** and paupers (poor people), and 30,000 vagrants (the criminal poor). As you will see in Section 3, life for these people lurched from hardship to famine, and they were treated very cruelly. King saw these people as a burden (as people who 'decreased the wealth of the kingdom').

Agriculture – 330,000 families

This section of society included rich 'yeoman' farmers down to small farmers.

Military – 94,000 families

In this category, King included officers, soldiers and seamen.

Activity

1 Put the information about society in 1696 from these pages into a graph or a drawing. Talk with a partner about the best way to present the figures – a pie chart? bar graph? population pyramid? Discuss your graph with your partner, and then explain to other students what it shows about society in 1696.
2 Consider these numbers: 50,000 commercial families, and 60,000 industrial families ... but 330,000 farming families, and 364,000 families of labourers – what does this tell you about England in 1696?
3 King lumped together working labourers with paupers and vagrants – what does this suggest about attitudes to poor people in 1696?

Studying the Early Modern Era

What do you know about the Tudors and Stuarts? Presumably you have heard of Henry VIII and his six wives, but you might not know also that we owe shopping malls and flushing toilets to the Early Modern Era.

As you study the different sections of this textbook, you will discover that the Early Modern Era was a vibrant, interesting and important period in British history. Here are ten of the headline events:

ARMADA DEFEATED (1588)

Bonnie Prince Charlie (1745)

First North American colony (1607)

First contact with India (1615)

First Poor Law (1601)

Glorious Revolution (1688)

Gunpowder Plot (1605)

KING CHARLES I BEHEADED (1649)

Start of the Church of England (1534)

Union with Scotland (1707)

Activity

Working as a whole class:

1 Have you heard of any of the headline events listed above? Share anything you think you know about any of them.

2 List together any other things you think you know about the Early Modern Era. Sort the list into two categories:

Facts (which we can prove right or wrong)	Ideas and interpretations (which are a matter of debate and opinion)

3 How did you find out the things you know about the Early Modern Era? What were the sources for your knowledge (e.g. books you have read – but there will be many others)?

4 When you have made a list, discuss for each item in turn how reliable and accurate you think they are as sources for a historian. Can you really trust anything you have learned from *any* of your sources?

... and now meet the historians

Different historians have come to different conclusions about the history of the Early Modern Era. In 1900, almost everybody would have told you that Britain was the 'land of hope and glory', with a great empire, a wonderful Parliament, and a marvellous Church of England – that was how most people thought in those days. So the people who wrote the history of Great Britain at that time came at the subject from a biased position, with the question: how did this (marvellous) state of affairs come into being?

Those historians developed what we call 'the **Whig Interpretation of History**'. For them, the Early Modern Era was especially important because, when they looked back, they traced the beginning of Great Britain's empire, Parliament and Church of England all to the sixteenth and seventeenth centuries. They decided that, in this period, Britain gradually, unstoppably and inevitably progressed towards the wealth, democracy and empire which they believed was her national destiny.

There is a lot wrong with the traditional Whig view of history. It is 'selective' – it chooses its facts to suit its theory. It is 'presentist' – it treats the past as though it is just a baby version of the present. It is 'triumphalistic', insisting that British history is just a series of leaps from one success to another.

Since the 1950s, **revisionist historians** have challenged and revised the claims of the Whig historians about the Early Modern Era.

Marxist historians interpreted the history of the Early Modern Era as part of a continual struggle for power between the classes – and they highlighted the history of ordinary people.

And **post-revisionist historians** – of which you are one – have decided that it is impossible to find 'the truth' about history ... and that the best we can do is to analyse the sources and develop interpretations, soundly based on evidence.

So now it is time for you to form your own interpretations of what happened. We're going to start with arguably the most famous person of all – Henry VIII.

Activity

5 Explain the four interpretations of history above in your own words. Do you agree that you are a post-revisionist historian?

Did Henry VIII live up to his public image?

You are going to continue your studies by investigating the reign of one of the most famous English kings in history – Henry VIII (1509–47).

Shortly before this section was written, two American computer scientists searched millions of pages of internet data to create a list of the most significant people in world history. Henry VIII came in at number eleven, the highest of any English monarch! Perhaps this is because Henry's decisions set the scene for the next 200 years of history.

This book will explore some of the issues resulting from Henry's reign. You will investigate bitter religious arguments, how the lives of

ordinary people changed over time, and how the United Kingdom was born. You will explore the relationship England had with the wider world and how power seemed to shift away from the monarchy towards parliament.

In this section you are going to look at what Henry VIII actually did, and decide: did Henry VIII live up to his public image? So let's begin by trying to find out just exactly what public image of himself Henry wanted to create.

A

⬆ The *Field of the Cloth of Gold* painted c.1545.

On 7 June 1520, cannons were heard not far from the French town of Calais. At this signal a hush descended on the small valley of the Val d'Or as the expectant crowd stood eerily still. King Francis I of France, one of the most powerful rulers in Europe, halted his men and looked toward the opposite slope. Facing him and surrounded by his nobles was King Henry VIII of England. Trumpets sounded as the two monarchs rode down the slopes towards one another. The crowds, warned to be still or face death, held their breath. The two kings embraced each other before dismounting and embracing once more. So began two weeks of singing, dancing, feasting and jousting. Francis resided in a magnificent golden pavilion but Henry entertained his guests in a spectacular palace. Yet on closer inspection Henry's palace was something of an illusion; the canvas roof was painted grey to look like lead, the high canvas walls were painted to resemble brick and stone.

Think

1 Can you find the French King's golden pavilion and Henry's canvas palace in painting A?
2 Discuss with a partner: What do you think Henry was trying to achieve with his canvas palace?

B

C

⬆ In 1521, King Henry wrote a book defending the Catholic Church from the criticisms of a German monk named Martin Luther (see pages 42–45). When the Pope read Henry's book he was so pleased that he awarded him the title 'Defender of the Faith'. Henry was the only ruler in Europe to be given this title. Therefore, he made sure it was widely known and it became an important part of his public image.

⬆ Henry clearly understood the importance of creating a positive public image. In 1537, he employed the Dutch artist Hans Holbein to paint his portrait. This is one of many copies.

Enquiry Step 1: First evidence – asking questions

Study pictures A–C. What image do you think Henry wanted to portray? For example, Henry's face shows an intelligent and wise expression in picture B. What does the rest of his body language suggest about him? What image do his clothes, jewels and dagger convey?

Make a list by adding to the suggestions made below:
▌ A wise and intelligent ruler.
▌ An important ruler in Europe.

'An auspicious star': the early years of Henry's reign

On pages 12–13 you saw what kind of king Henry tried to portray himself as. Now you can start to decide whether the reality matched the image.

Henry's father (Henry VII 1485–1509) had been a serious man and was careful not to spend too much money. This meant that the treasury was full and the country rich when his son came to the throne.

Henry the scholar

Henry VIII enjoyed an excellent education and spoke French, Latin and Spanish. He was also a talented musician, able to play a range of instruments, sing and even compose his own pieces. There was huge excitement when he became king.

Henry the sportsman

The young king was a natural athlete and sportsman. Foreign visitors to his **court** described him as a gifted archer and tennis player but it was hunting that really excited Henry. He could tire as many as eight horses a day before finally running out of steam. Jousting and wrestling tournaments were also favourite pastimes and Henry was regarded as a strong and fearsome opponent.

Henry the spender

Along with royal tournaments, Henry spent huge sums of money on pageants, feasts and other entertainments. Unlike his father, Henry had a taste for luxury and made little attempt to control his spending. He paid vast sums for building work and decoration to improve his various royal palaces. Henry also wore only the finest clothes and jewellery. By the mid-1520s, the extra money his father had left in the treasury was all used up!

D

⬆ Portrait of Henry VIII in 1509, by an unknown artist.

E

When you know what a hero he now shows himself, how wisely he behaves, what a lover of justice and goodness, what affection he bears to the learned, I will venture to swear that you will need no wings to make you fly to behold this new and auspicious star.

Lord Mountjoy, a leading advisor of the king, writing in 1509 to his old teacher, just after Henry had become king.

> **Think**
>
> Working with a partner, look at who wrote extract E. Do you trust this source to give you a reliable description of the king? Explain your thinking.

Henry the general

Henry was greatly impressed by the achievements of King Henry V (1386–1422) who had won the Battle of Agincourt in 1415, despite being heavily outnumbered by the French. Unfortunately, King Henry VIII was not very skilled as a general. In 1513 he tried to re-conquer long lost land in France; he defeated the French army at the Battle of the Spurs, but his invasion ended in failure.

There were some successes in his reign. During Henry's first campaign in France, in 1513, the Scots invaded the North of England. Henry's wife Catherine organised an army, which totally defeated them.

F

⬆ The ship *Henry Grace of God*, built in 1514, was armed with 43 heavy cannons and 141 **swivel guns**. The ship was top-heavy and almost unsailable in heavy seas. It never fought in a battle, but was used for show (such as taking Henry VIII to his meeting with Francis I at the Field of the Cloth of Gold – see page 12).

Henry also understood the need for England to have a powerful navy and increased the fleet to fifty ships. He spent money on large cannons that could be used in ship-to-ship battles, a more effective tactic than attempting to board and capture enemy ships. Work was done to improve ports and dockyards around the country and Henry ordered the building of a string of fortresses to defend the English coast. Some historians have called Henry the father of the modern navy.

Enquiry Step 2: Suggesting an answer

1 Working in a small group, copy the table below and use the evidence on pages 14 and 15 to decide whether – in the early years of his reign – Henry lived up to the public image he wanted to give. Score Henry out of ten but make sure you give your reasons and evidence in the final column. (You won't be able to fill in the entire table yet – there is more information to look at in the next few pages.)

Public image	Score /10	Evidence for your score
Henry was an intelligent and wise ruler		
Henry was wealthy and ensured the country was prosperous		
Henry was able to win wars and keep the country safe		
Henry was a powerful ruler		
Henry was a **pious** ruler who would defend the faith		

2 Based on the information you have gathered so far, did Henry live up to the public image he wanted to create for himself?

The succession question and the break with Rome

Henry longed for a son who would inherit the throne when he died. This had a huge effect on Henry's actions and on those closest to him. It would also have far-reaching consequences for the whole of England.

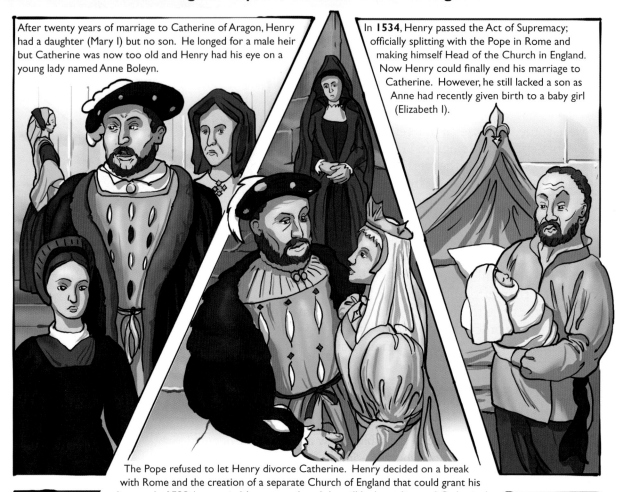

After twenty years of marriage to Catherine of Aragon, Henry had a daughter (Mary I) but no son. He longed for a male heir but Catherine was now too old and Henry had his eye on a young lady named Anne Boleyn.

In 1534, Henry passed the Act of Supremacy; officially splitting with the Pope in Rome and making himself Head of the Church in England. Now Henry could finally end his marriage to Catherine. However, he still lacked a son as Anne had recently given birth to a baby girl (Elizabeth I).

The Pope refused to let Henry divorce Catherine. Henry decided on a break with Rome and the creation of a separate Church of England that could grant his divorce. In 1533, he married Anne even though he still had not divorced Catherine!

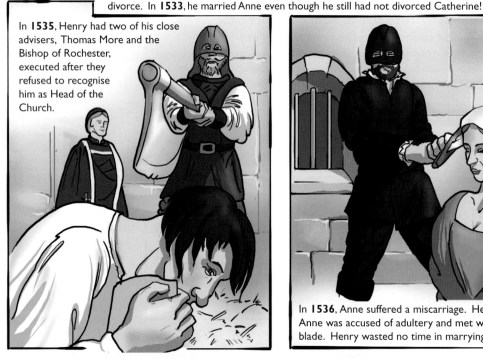

In 1535, Henry had two of his close advisers, Thomas More and the Bishop of Rochester, executed after they refused to recognise him as Head of the Church.

In 1536, Anne suffered a miscarriage. Henry lost patience. Anne was accused of adultery and met with the executioner's blade. Henry wasted no time in marrying again.

In 1537, Henry's new wife Jane Seymour gave him the son he longed for (Edward VI) but she died after childbirth.

In 1540, Henry married Anne of Cleves in an attempt to ally England with the Protestant Duchy of Cleves against Catholic France and Spain. Henry had only ever seen portraits of Anne — when he saw her in person he disliked her appearance so much that he soon divorced her.

Henry's next wife was Catherine Howard. She was young and pretty and the marriage in 1540 helped Henry win the support of the powerful Duke of Norfolk. However, Catherine was accused of adultery and in 1542 she was executed along with her lovers.

In 1543, Henry married his sixth wife, Catherine Parr. She nursed Henry through various illnesses and outlived him when he died in 1547.

Enquiry Step 3: Developing your answer

1 Working in your group, discuss the evidence on pages 16 and 17 to decide whether Henry lived up to the public image he wanted to give. Did his conduct here match the image of the wise, powerful and pious monarch Henry claimed to be?

Remember the table you drew for Enquiry Step 2 (page 15)? For each aspect of Henry's public image decide whether you want to adjust the score out of ten you gave him. Make sure you add your reasons and evidence to the final column.

2 Based on the information you have gathered so far, did Henry live up to the public image he wanted to create for himself?

The dissolution of the monasteries

On pages 18–19, we look at Henry's behaviour after 1536, continuing our study of whether he lived up to his public image.

Between 1536 and 1540 Henry closed down all of the **monasteries** in England – an action known as the dissolution of the monasteries. This was partly because monks and nuns were supposed to be loyal to the Pope as leader of the Catholic Church, and not to Henry. Secondly, some were no longer leading spiritual lives and had become corrupt. However, the closures were mainly due to Henry's desperate need for money caused by his extravagant spending.

> **Think**
>
> What do Henry's actions suggest about his attitude to religion? Was he the pious ruler he claimed to be?

Some monasteries had valuable items such as gold crosses, cups and other treasures. Even the buildings could be stripped down: the stone blocks and the lead from the roof could all be sold.

Some monasteries owned huge amounts of land. This allowed them to grow wealthy through the collection of rents. By seizing this land, Henry was able to double his yearly income and for a time he became the richest ruler in Europe.

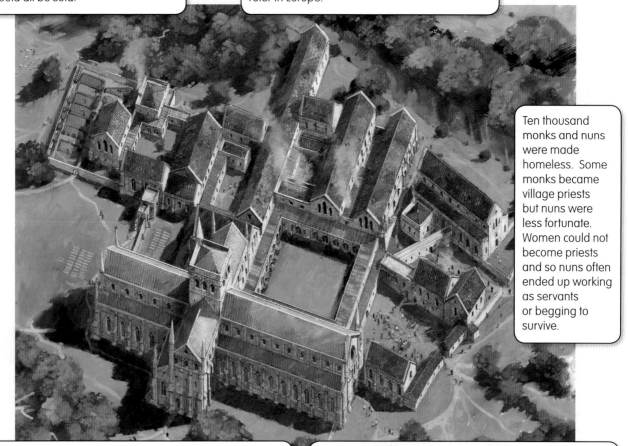

Ten thousand monks and nuns were made homeless. Some monks became village priests but nuns were less fortunate. Women could not become priests and so nuns often ended up working as servants or begging to survive.

Monasteries had sometimes helped care for the sick and needy and these people now had nowhere else to turn. Begging and homelessness increased as a result.

In 1536, there was an uprising in Lincolnshire. People were angry at the closures. Henry dealt with it ruthlessly. Despite promising to consider their complaints, Henry ordered that the leaders and 200 protesters be executed.

Henry's final years

As Henry grew older, he grew fatter and more irritable. He developed an ulcer on his leg, after a jousting accident, which leaked pus and caused him agony. Some historians think this may help to explain why Henry became even more brutal towards the end of his reign. In 1540, he executed Thomas Cromwell, one of his most trusted ministers. In 1542 his fifth wife, Catherine Howard, suffered the same fate.

Henry had helped establish the authority of Parliament by using it to pass his laws. However, in 1539 a new law – the Statute of Proclamations – made it clear that Henry's authority was only second to God and that his grip on power was very strong. It allowed him to pass any law that he wanted without having to involve Parliament. In the same year, Henry passed the Six Articles, which sentenced anyone who denied the central beliefs of the Catholic Church to death by burning. Henry was clearly not a Protestant like Martin Luther (see pages 40–44). However, this did not stop him having his son Edward educated by Protestant advisers.

Henry united Wales with England in 1536, and declared himself the ruler of Ireland in 1541. In 1544, during a second war with France, Henry managed to capture the city of Boulogne. Despite the celebrations, this was no great victory. The cost of war left England nearly bankrupt. All of the money raised from the dissolution of the monasteries had been wasted on another unsuccessful war.

Henry died in 1547. Some say he departed with the name of Jane Seymour, his favourite wife, on his lips but others claim he cried out 'Monks! Monks!'

Henry's reign was to 'set the scene' for the next two centuries … and for the rest of this textbook!

Enquiry Step 4: Concluding your enquiry

1 Working in your group, discuss the evidence on pages 18–19 to decide whether you want to adjust the scores out of ten you gave Henry in Enquiry Step 3 for how well he lived up to his public image. Make sure you add your reasons and evidence to the final column of your table.
2 Coming together as a whole class, compare your final scores with other groups' judgements. In which areas did you score Henry the highest? Where did you score him the lowest? Discuss this carefully.
3 Now that you have looked at all of the evidence in this chapter, write an information panel to go next to the painting of Henry VIII on page 13 in answer to the enquiry question:

Did Henry VIII live up to his public image?

Use the sentence starters below to help you write your panel:

1 Henry VIII had a clear idea of the kind of image he wanted to create …

(Look back at the list you made in Enquiry Step 1 on page 13.)

2 In some ways, Henry did live up to his image …

(Use the table you completed in this Enquiry Step to give examples.)

3 However, in other ways Henry did not live up to his image …

(Use the table you completed in this Enquiry Step to give examples.)

4 Overall, I think Henry did/did not live up to his public image because …

(Make your own judgement and give your reasons.)

Did life get better, 1509–1745?

	Medieval life and society, 1066–1509	Tudor life and society, 1509–1603
1	Medieval warm period; generally good harvests.	Falling temperatures; failed harvests and famines towards the end of the period.
2	Low prices, high wages.	Rapidly rising prices; wages lagging behind.
3	The cloth trade.	The cloth trade.
4	Horses, with clumsy carriages and carts.	Horses, with clumsy carriages and carts.
5	The **Black Death**; doctors could not cure disease. Average height: 170cm. Population: 2.5 million.	The sweating sickness; doctors could not cure disease. Average height: 170cm. Population: 3 million.
6	Fortified manor houses for the rich; wattle and daub hovels for the poor.	Wealthy stately homes for the rich; wattle and daub hovels for the poor.
7	For the rich, huge feasts with many courses, mainly of meat; the poor lived on broth and bread.	For the rich, huge feasts with many courses, mainly of meat; the poor lived on broth and bread.
8	Religious festivals and miracle plays, hunting.	Theatre, football, bear-baiting, executions.
9	Monasteries for the poor.	Poor Laws of 1572 and 1601 – **out-relief** for the impotent poor; punishment for vagrants.

Activity

1 As you can see, the table rows on pages 20–21 split 'life and society' into nine different categories. Come up with a title for each category.
2 Split the class into nine groups. Each group takes a different category and decides: did life in this area improve through the ages? Explain your decision and support it with facts.

Stuart life and society, 1603–1714	Georgian life and society, 1714–45
Little Ice Age; failed harvests and famines.	Little Ice Age; failed harvests and famines.
Prices rising, but wages rose only slowly.	Prices stable; but wages rose only slowly.
First colonies; trade in sugar, tobacco, tea and slaves.	First steam engine; beginnings of the Industrial Revolution.
Horses, with carriages and carts.	Stage coaches, canals and some good 'turnpike' roads.
Bubonic Plague; doctors could not cure disease. Average height: 166cm. Population: 5 million.	Typhus and malaria; doctors could not cure disease. Average height: 166cm. Population: 6 million.
Elegant stately homes for the rich; damp, cold cottages for the poor.	Elegant terraced town houses for the rich; rotting slums for the poor.
For the rich, huge feasts with many courses, mainly of meat with some vegetables; the poor lived on broth and bread.	For the rich, huge feasts with many courses, mainly of meat with some vegetables, tea and coffee; the poor lived on broth, bread … and gin.
Theatre, cricket, horse-racing and gambling.	Theatre, cricket, horse-racing and gambling.
Out-relief for the impotent poor; punishment for vagrants.	Workhouses for the poor.

Activity

3 Coming together as a whole class, share your findings from Activity 2, then discuss and decide:
- Taking all the information together, does it seem that life got better as the years went by?
- What other information would you have wanted to know about to study the quality of people's lives?
- Does the information on these pages prove that life got better?

What can pictures tell us about whether life got better?

When you studied the Middle Ages and investigated what life was like for ordinary people, what were your conclusions? This artist's recreation of Wharram Percy in North Yorkshire gives a powerful impression of what life was like in the Middle Ages. Life was not wholly bad – but people were poor, they depended on growing their own food, and if harvests were bad or disease struck people could suffer terribly. In this section, you are going to extend your study of 'everyday life' into the Early Modern Era.

The 'Whig' view

The Early Modern Era (1509–1745), started with England emerging from the Middle Ages, and ended with the United Kingdom on the cusp of an **Industrial Revolution** and world empire. If you had asked the '**Whig**' historians of the early twentieth century, therefore, if everyday life had improved, they would have regarded the question as a 'no-brainer'. Of course life improved, they would have told you.

In this section, you are going to revisit the evidence and decide for yourself whether the Whig historians were right – did life get better in the Early Modern Era? Many modern historians would question whether life for everyone improved continuously between 1509 and 1745.

You are going to begin by analysing contemporary pictures of life at three points in the period – 1559, 1640 and 1750 – to see what they might tell us about how life changed in the Early Modern Era.

A

Activity

Working with a partner or in a small group, study picture A.

1 What does it tell you about:
- buildings and architecture
- clothing and fashions
- jobs
- amusements and leisure
in Tudor times?
- wealth and poverty
- cleanliness and health
- transport

2 What impression does picture A give of the quality of life in 1559?

3 From the evidence in picture A alone, would you agree that life in 1559 was an improvement on everyday life in the Middle Ages?

Everyday life in 1559

Think

What are the limitations of picture A as evidence to tell us what life was like in England in 1559?

↑ This painting by Pieter Bruegel (1559) shows a street scene in Holland during a carnival. Bruegel was a Dutch painter, but his pictures are often used to convey an impression of what life was like in Tudor England. It is important to realise that this is a comic painting.

Everyday life in 1640

This woodcut, entitled *The Severall* ➡ **B** *Places Where you May hear News*, shows various scenes from everyday life in seventeenth-century London. This version is dated 1640.

It is important to realise that the drawing is anti-women – it is based on a sixteenth-century French picture called 'The clucking of women'.

Activity

Working with a partner or in a small group, study picture B.
1 What does it tell you about:
  ▪ buildings and architecture
  ▪ clothing and fashions
  ▪ jobs
  ▪ amusements and leisure
  ▪ wealth and poverty
  ▪ cleanliness and health
  ▪ transport
  in London in 1640?
2 What impression does picture B give of the quality of life in 1640?
3 From the evidence in picture B alone, would you agree that life in 1640 was an improvement on everyday life in 1559 (picture A, pages 22–23)?

Think

What are the limitations of picture B as evidence to tell us what life was like in England in 1640?

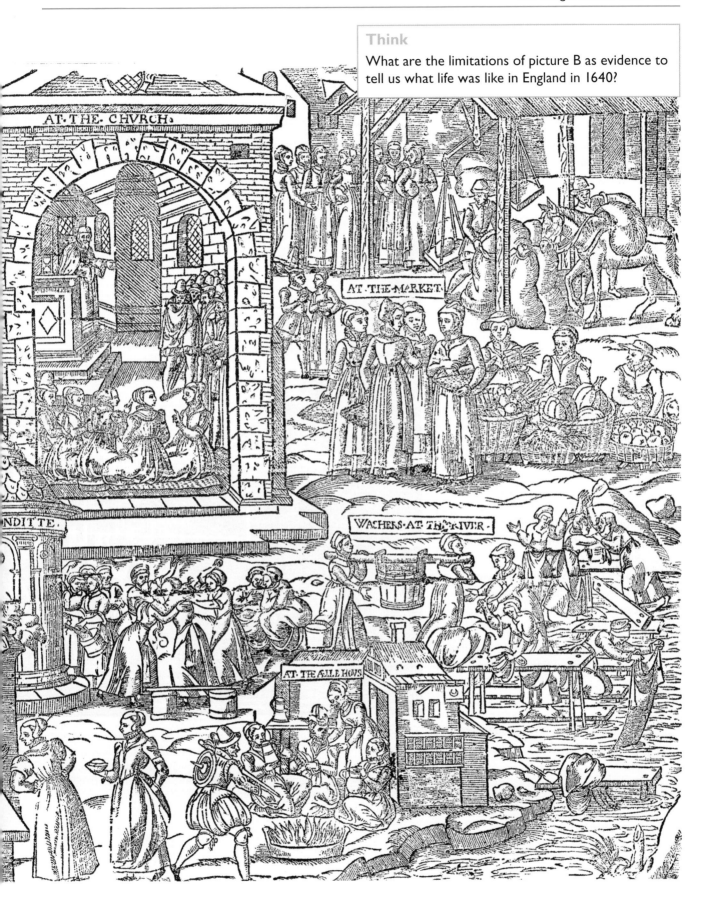

Everyday life in 1750

Activity

Working with a partner or in a small group, study picture C.

1 What does it tell you about:
 ▌ buildings and architecture
 ▌ clothing and fashions
 ▌ jobs
 ▌ amusements and leisure
 ▌ wealth and poverty
 ▌ cleanliness and health
 ▌ transport

 in London in 1750?

2 What impression does picture C give of the quality of life in 1750?

3 From the evidence in picture C alone, would you agree that life in 1750 was an improvement on everyday life in 1640 (picture B, pages 24–25)?

4 Coming together as a whole class, share your ideas about pictures A, B and C and discuss the following.
 ▌ Do pictures A, B and C give an impression that everyday life improved steadily during the period 1509–1745, as the Whig historians claimed?
 ▌ Do pictures A, B and C prove that everyday life improved continuously during the period 1509–1745?

5 What other evidence would you like to see before deciding whether life improved between 1509 and 1745?

Think

What are the limitations of picture C as evidence to tell us what life was like in England in 1750?

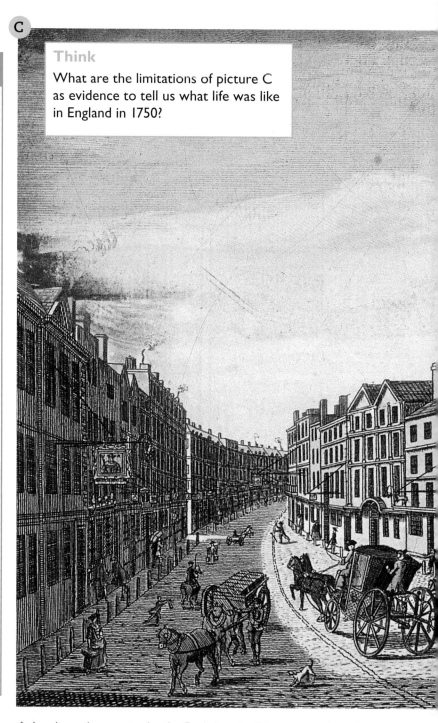

⬆ A coloured engraving by the English artist Thomas Bowles, of Fenchurch Street in London showing the Ironmongers' Hall. It is a 'perspective' print which, when viewed through a double convex lens, gives the viewer a 3D impression of the street. The Bowles family owned a printing business and sold prints of London landmarks to tourists.

6 Having studied pictures A, B and C, what is your starting opinion?

| I am convinced by the evidence that things got better | The balance of evidence seems to be for improvement | Unsure – I am unconvinced by the evidence either way | The balance of evidence is that things did not improve | I am convinced by the evidence that things did not get better |

Explain your decision. Record your decision and the reasons for it.

What can statistics tell us about whether life got better?

After studying pages 22–27, you probably decided that pictures A, B and C supported the Whig historians' claim that life improved between 1509 and 1745 ... but you suspected that the pictures (and therefore your conclusions) only showed part of the story. In the rest of this section, therefore, we will approach the question of whether life got better in different ways, to see whether they support or contradict the Whig interpretation.

The easiest answer to the 'did life get better' question, of course, would be if we had a *statistical* way to measure people's quality of life. Nowadays, we use a measure called 'real wages' – the *buying power* of people's wages – to measure what we call their '**standard of living**'.

No one kept good enough statistics in the Early Modern Era for us to be able to calculate real wages for those times. However, in the 1950s, two economic historians, Henry Phelps-Brown and Sheila Hopkins, compared data about builders' wages across seven centuries with prices, and came up with this graph:

D

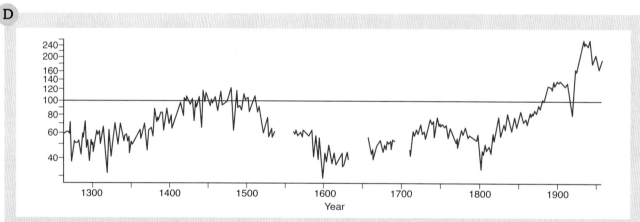

Phelps-Brown and Hopkins (1956): *Index of Changes in the Equivalent of the Wage Rate of a Building Craftsman.*

The graph shows the buying power of builders' wages, 1264–1954 (gaps in the line represent missing data). Phelps-Brown and Hopkins calculated the values for the graph by seeing how much builders' wages in the south-east of England would buy given the prices at the time. The figures are presented as percentages, where 1451 = 100%. Thus, for instance, builders' wages in 1597 and 1797 could barely buy 30 per cent (less than a third) of what they could in 1451.

Activity

1 Working with a partner or in a small group, draw a rough copy of graph D. Label your copy to identify:
- the Early Modern Era 1509–1745
- the famines of 1597 and 1797
- the economic crash of the 1930s
- the growth in people's real wages after the Black Death of 1348–50
- the growth in real wages during the later Industrial Revolution 1850–1900.

Then discuss the following questions.
a) In what years were builders relatively rich? When were they poor?
b) Prices rose rapidly during the sixteenth century; what effect did this have on real wages?
c) What does the graph suggest about living standards, 1509–1745?

Another statistical data-set is skeletal height.

Builders' wages and skeletal height are known as 'proxy' statistics – data *closely connected* to the matter we want to measure, and which tell us something about what was going on. So table E, for example, provides proxy data for the standard of living question because wealthier people will eat better, be healthier and therefore grow taller.

E

Date	Height (cm)	Source
1200–1400	170	174 archaeological remains (Midlands)
1510	170	90 remains of the crew of the Mary Rose
1650–1750	166	443 archaeological remains (London)
1762–89	172	167 army records
1800s	164	7055 historical records
1830s	173	10,863 historical records
1970s	178	Military and medical data

The height of male skeletons in England.

Activity

2 Working with a partner or in a small group, draw a graph of the data in table E.
- ▊ Discuss what your graph suggests about living standards 1509–1745.
- ▊ Compare it to the real wages data in graph D.

3 Coming together as a whole class:
- ▊ Discuss the graphs and make a list of THREE tentative conclusions you might draw about the standard of living in the Early Modern Era, 1509–1745.
- ▊ List the limitations of graph D and table E as evidence.
- ▊ Suggest things that statistics like these cannot tell us about the quality of people's lives.
- ▊ Is there a difference between 'the standard of living' and 'the quality of life'? Devise a convincing argument that statistics are almost worthless for historians wanting to study the quality of life in the Early Modern Era.

4 You started this chapter acknowledging that there was evidence which suggested but did not prove the Whig claim that there was a steady improvement in everyday life, 1509–1745. Has what you have learned from builders' wages and the height of skeletons caused you to change your position in the debate?
- ▊ Do graph D and table E support the Whig claim that living standards steadily improved?
- ▊ Do graph D and table E prove that living standards did not improve?

Having considered the statistical evidence, what is your opinion now on the debate?

| I am convinced by the evidence that things got better | The balance of evidence seems to be for improvement | Unsure – I am unconvinced by the evidence either way | The balance of evidence is that things did not improve | I am convinced by the evidence that things did not get better |

Explain your decision. Record your revised position and the reasons for it.

Did better farming methods improve people's lives?

It could be argued that population is the ultimate proxy indicator of whether people's lives were getting better – if the population was increasing, surely that suggests that the country was getting wealthier!

Farming makes food!

Children at school in the 1960s were taught that the 'agricultural revolution' occurred in the late eighteenth century, and that it was based on clover, turnips, manure and enclosing the land into private farms (which replaced the old inefficient medieval open fields).

By the 1970s, all that had changed. An 'agricultural revolution', had started well before 1750. King Henry VIII ate turnips, clover came to England in 1633, and **enclosure** had been happening since the sixteenth century!

As early as 1652, Walter Blith's *Improver Improved* was recommending putting manure on the fields. And about 1701 the first seed drill was invented by Jethro Tull. It not only hid the seed from the birds by planting it in the soil, but sowed the seed in straight lines – which allowed farmers for the first time to weed their crops effectively.

In the period 1509–1745, therefore, agriculture improved (as graph F below shows), better farming meant more food ... and England's population more than doubled. Can it be argued that this proves that life improved in the Early Modern Era?

F

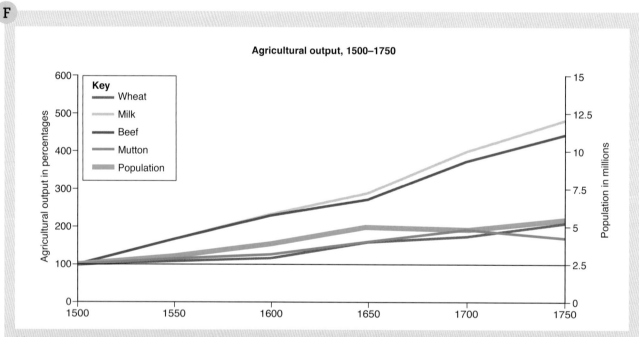

No records were kept at the time. The figures for agricultural output (marked on the left-hand side of the graph) come from estimates made by a team of expert economic historians in 2009; they are presented (like the figures for real wages on page 28) as a percentage of the amount produced in 1500 – so more than four times as much beef was produced in 1750 than in 1500. The population figures, marked on the right-hand side of the graph, are also estimates. The key output was wheat, which was made into bread – the staple food, especially for the poor. What do you notice about the production of wheat, compared to population, in the Early Modern Era?

In fact, an 'agricultural revolution' does not necessarily mean that life was getting better.

1. Inequality of wealth

Increased food production does not always mean more food for everyone. Throughout the period, the poor remained desperately ill-fed.

2. Enclosure riots

Enclosure caused great hardship for the rural poor because it meant they couldn't hunt or grow food on common land as this land was now privately owned. There was a major rebellion against enclosures (Kett's Rebellion) in Norfolk in 1549, and many riots and smaller uprisings throughout the period.

3. The Little Ice Age

You saw on page 6 that the weather was generally much colder in the Early Modern Era. But colder, wetter weather also ruined the harvest more often, leading to regular food shortages and famines.

4. The population ceiling

Just as in the Middle Ages, people remained at the mercy of bad harvests and disease throughout the period. When the population increased too quickly a bad harvest led to deaths from starvation and underfed people fell ill and died more easily.

The **sweating sickness** hit England in a series of epidemics between 1485 and 1551. There were also regular outbreaks of **bubonic plague** every ten years or so throughout the period; the last – the Great Plague of London in 1665 – killed perhaps 200,000 people.

A particularly bad year occurred in England in 1729 when the harvest failed for the third year running and there was an influenza epidemic. The death rate that year rose by two-thirds.

Activity

1 Give graph F a more appropriate title. Working in a small group, write a paragraph to explain what the graph seems to show about farming and the population in the years 1509–1745. Did life get better during this period?

2 ▌ Pictures A, B and C (on pages 22–27) gave the impression, but did not prove, that life got steadily better.
   ▌ Graph D and table E (pages 28–29) indicated, but did not prove, that the standard of living fell.
   ▌ The information on these pages, 30–31, must have given you mixed messages about whether or not life got better. Working in your group:
   a) List the information on these pages which suggests that life was getting better.
   b) List the information on these pages which suggests that life was not getting better.

3 Having considered the information about farming and population, what is your opinion now on the debate?

I am convinced by the evidence that things got better	The balance of evidence seems to be for improvement	Unsure – I am unconvinced by the evidence either way	The balance of evidence is that things did not improve	I am convinced by the evidence that things did not get better

Explain your decision. Record your revised position and the reasons for it.

Did increasing trade and industry improve people's lives?

Towards the end of our period, another development took place which we must consider when we are thinking about whether life got better. After 1688 there was a marked and quickening growth in the economy.

Mostly this involved a growth of trade – in luxury goods such as sugar (from the West Indies), tobacco (from North America) and tea (from India), but especially in the **slave trade**.

However, the economy in general was also growing, as shown by inventions such as Newcomen's Steam Engine (1712), Kay's Flying Shuttle (to speed up weaving, 1733) and Darby's blast furnace (which made iron using coke, 1709).

Activity

I Study picture G. List FIVE different kinds of economic activity and FIVE signs of wealth you can see in the painting. Can you spot the black servant boy in the picture – evidence which reminds us that much of Bristol's wealth was linked to the slave trade?

G

⬆ A painting of Broad Quay, Bristol in 1735 by the Dutch immigrant Philip Vandyke, who had settled in the city.

Growing wealth?

The Whig historians looked at Britain's growing economy, and simply assumed that if Britain was getting wealthier, so were the people. But is this inevitably true?

In 1727 Daniel Defoe published a *Tour thro' the whole island of Great Britain*. He wrote the book, he explained, because he was fed up with 'some foreigners' who had 'very ill reports of the land'. Instead, he promised the reader 'a description of the most flourishing and opulent country in the world … the improvement, as well in culture, as in commerce, the encrease of people, and employment for them'.

This is how he described two areas: the West Riding of Yorkshire and the Peak District in Derbyshire.

H

Cloth-makers in the West Riding

We found the country one continued village … hardly a house standing out of a speaking distance from another … in which dwell the workmen which are employed, the women and children of whom, are always busy **carding**, spinning, etc., so that no hands being unemploy'd, all can gain their bread, even from the youngest to the antient; hardly any thing above four years old, but its hands are sufficient to it self.

This is the reason also why we saw so few people out doors; but if we knock'd at the door of any of the master manufacturers, we saw a house full of lusty fellows, some dyeing the cloth, some in the loom, all hard at work and full employed.

I

A lead miner's home in Derbyshire

There was a large hollow cave, which the poor people, by two curtains hang'd cross, had parted into three rooms.

The habitation was poor, 'tis true, but things within did not look so like misery as I expected. Every thing was clean and neat, tho' mean and ordinary: There were shelves with earthen ware, and some pewter and brass. There was, which I observed in particular, a whole side of bacon hanging up in the chimney.

There was a sow and pigs running about at the door, and a little lean cow feeding upon a green place just before the door, and a little enclosed piece of ground was growing with good barley.

Activity

2 Working with a partner or in a small group, study the information on pages 32 and 33, then:
   ▌ Find all the evidence you can that England grew wealthier, 1688–1745.
   ▌ Did life get better for EVERYONE as a result of the Commercial Revolution?
3 Can we wholly trust Daniel Defoe's descriptions?
4 Has this information about trade and industry changed your position in the debate about whether life got better in the period 1509–1745? Where do you stand now?

| I am convinced by the evidence that things got better | The balance of evidence seems to be for improvement | Unsure – I am unconvinced by the evidence either way | The balance of evidence is that things did not improve | I am convinced by the evidence that things did not get better |

Explain your decision. Record your revised position and the reasons for it.

Did life get better for the poor?

It is often said that the way to judge a society is to look at how it treats its poor people ... so for the next part of our enquiry we will look at whether society started to treat its weakest and most vulnerable members any better, 1509–1745.

Tudor welfare

Until 1536, the monasteries provided charity for the poor (see page 18). So Henry VIII's dissolution of the monasteries set the government a problem – what to do with all the poor people?

At first, the government simply punished them. Henry VIII's law of 1536 ordered that they be whipped. A 1547 Act of Edward VI sentenced them to two years' hard labour and branding with a 'V' (for 'vagrant') ... and death if they ran away! The problem with this law was that it was so harsh that few magistrates ever enforced it.

So it was the Poor Law Act of 1572, in the reign of Elizabeth I (1558–1603), which was the turning point. It still set punishments for 'rogues, vagabonds and sturdy beggars'. But it also, for the first time in English history, distinguished between them and the 'impotent poor' – unfortunate people who were too old or weak to work. And, instead of punishing the poor, it ordered the **Justice of the Peace** to collect **rates** from local people to support them (see extract J).

The Old Poor Law

By the end of Elizabeth's reign, poor people were suffering from the rapidly rising prices, especially of food and fuel. Cold weather and failed harvests led to famines in certain parts of the country.

In 1601, therefore, Parliament passed an Act for the Relief of the Poor which made it the job of the local parishes to look after the poor – the impotent poor were to be given **out-relief**, the able-bodied poor were to be forced to work in a **workhouse**, and the idle poor were to be punished.

From the beginning of the eighteenth century, many parishes began to build workhouses for their poor. In 1723 Parliament passed the Workhouse Test Act, which allowed parishes to join together to afford to build them. By 1776 there were almost 2000 workhouses in England and Wales, housing about 100,000 paupers. Often these workhouses put the elderly, infirm and orphans in one wing, and petty criminals and vagrants in another.

J

The Poor Law Act of 1572

Where all the parts of the realm of England and Wales be presently exceedingly pestered with rogues, vagabonds and sturdy beggars, by means whereof daily happeneth horrible murders, thefts and other outrages, be it enacted that all persons above the age of fourteen years, being rogues, vagabonds or sturdy beggars ... shall be grievously whipped and burnt through the gristle of the right ear with a hot iron.

And forasmuch as charity would that poor aged and impotent persons should necessarily be provided for [and] have habitations and abiding places to the end that they nor any of them should hereafter beg or wander about; it is therefore enacted that the **Justices of the Peace** shall make a register book of the names and surnames of all aged poor, impotent and decayed persons ... and shall tax all and every the inhabitants to such weekly charge as they and every of them shall weekly contribute towards the relief of the said poor people.

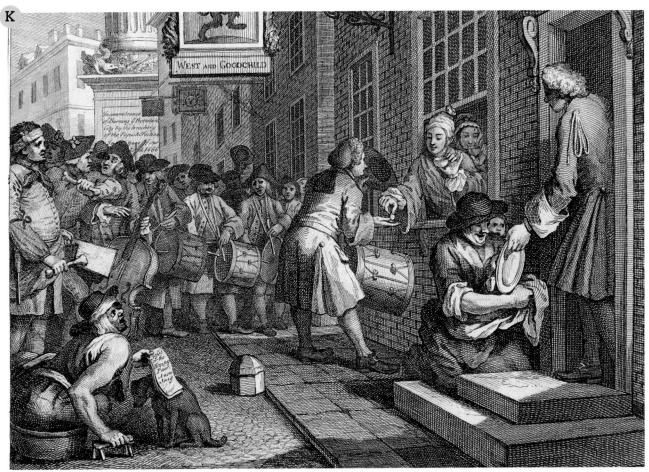

⬆ This 1747 engraving is from a set of prints by William Hogarth called *Industry and Idleness*. The hard-working man – 'Francis Goodchild' – has just finished his apprenticeship and married the boss' daughter. Their wedding feast is disrupted by a crowd of poor people. Francis gives a street musician a coin; his servant gives an old woman a plate. 'Philip' – the man with no legs sitting in a tub – waves a street-ballad for sale.

Activity

1 Make a list of the SEVEN key dates in the development of the Poor Law; do you agree that 'the turning point' was 1572?

2 Working in a small group, study extract J and picture K.

▎ What does extract J tell you about poverty and people's attitudes to it in Tudor times?

▎ What does picture K tell you about poverty and people's attitudes to it in the eighteenth century?

3 Share your findings as a whole class – were the poor better treated in 1745 than they were in 1509?

4 Has this information about the treatment of poor people changed your position in the debate about whether life got better in the period 1509–1745? Where do you stand now?

| I am convinced by the evidence that things got better | The balance of evidence seems to be for improvement | Unsure – I am unconvinced by the evidence either way | The balance of evidence is that things did not improve | I am convinced by the evidence that things did not get better |

Explain your decision. Record your revised position and the reasons for it.

35

Concluding your enquiry: Did life get better, 1509–1745?

We will finish our enquiry on whether life got better by looking at some evidence in two pictures by William Hogarth – then we will discover some problems with the Whig view of prosperity on the following pages.

This 1743 oil painting by William Hogarth is from a series entitled *Marriage à la Mode*, and shows a rich woman (on the right) holding her morning reception. Notice the following details:

- The crown over the bed, which shows that her husband is an earl.
- The famous opera singer and flautist who have been hired to entertain the guests.
- The man with the blue coat and curlers in his hair – a German diplomat.
- The black servant and page boy.
- The cards on the floor, indicating that she is wasteful with money.
- The hideous ornaments on the floor which she has recently bought.
- The red rope of coral hung over the back of her chair, used as a teething ring – the lady is a mother, but her baby is not with her.
- The paintings on the wall are all about sex and seduction (the lady is having an affair with the man in the black coat – how does Hogarth show that he is too familiar with her?).

M

This 1751 engraving by William Hogarth – an allegory on the social damage caused by alcohol – shows a scene in 'Gin Lane' in London. Notice the following details:

- The (very meaningful) name of the gin distiller at the top right.
- The mother feeding gin to her baby.
- The saw – essential to his trade – being pawned by a carpenter.
- The gin cellar, with the promise: 'Drunk for a penny, dead drunk for two pence, clean straw for nothing'.
- The black dog – a symbol of depression – and the snail – a symbol of laziness.

Activity

1 Make a list of all the signs of wealth and excess you can see in picture L, and all the signs of poverty and despair you can see in picture M.

2 Share your results as a whole class. Why does the vast gap between rich and poor make it difficult for historians to judge whether living standards had improved since Tudor times?

The Whig view – did life get better, 1509–1745?

When Mr Clare was at school in the 1960s, all the textbooks accepted without question the 'Whig' view of gradual but continuous improvement in life during the Early Modern Era – that was why they called it the 'Early Modern Era', because it seemed that, during these years, the foundations of our modern lifestyle and prosperity had been laid.

The issue

When you began to study this section, you started with three sources (pages 22–27) which gave the same impression – of significant, steady improvements in buildings and architecture, clothing and fashions, amusements and leisure, wealth, cleanliness and health, and transport.

On pages 28–37, however, you have been making enquiries into different aspects of the topic, which should have left you with the impression that the answer to the question is far from clear-cut!

Your study of statistics found that in the Early Modern Era real wages were at their lowest (and people at their smallest in height) in six centuries. Then your study of farming and population revealed that there was, throughout the period, a **population ceiling** of famine and disease (pages 30–31).

Your study of the Commercial Revolution (pages 32–33) showed that there was a quickening of economic activity after 1688 which seems to have extended to the working classes. But, when you studied the poor (pages 34–35), you saw that the most vulnerable members of society were treated little better in 1745 than they had been in 1509.

It is time to pull together your various notes and thoughts and to write a report on whether life got better, 1509–1745, but first we will look at some problems.

Some problems

Measuring change

How can you measure changes in the quality of people's lives across a period of 250 years? One change, for example, was that people stopped jousting and started playing cricket. People living in 1745 probably thought cricket was much better than jousting and so much more civilised … but would a person living in 1509 have been happier being made to play cricket rather than jousting?

Measuring happiness

So how do you measure happiness? How do you compare things such as feelings, hopes and fears? Did people notice smells in the same way? The famous playwright William Shakespeare (1564–1616) wrote his plays in the reigns of Elizabeth I and James I; but when he talked of 'love', did he mean the same feeling as the playwrights who wrote about love 150 years later?

Class differences

What about the difference between rich and poor, as you saw on pages 36 and 37? How can you be sure that you are not just comparing poor people in one period with rich people in another? Does it become a matter of numbers – how many rich and poor people?

Trusting the sources

Can we trust the sources – do you think, for example, that there was anywhere in London as bad as Gin Lane (picture M, page 37) – or was the artist (William Hogarth) trying to make a moral point by exaggeration?

Activity

3 Organise and hold a class debate on the question

Did life get better, 1509–1745?

To do this, the class splits into two – half the pupils will advocate the idea that everyday life got steadily better during the Early Modern Era, the other half will argue that the period was not a story of unbroken progress. Each side should spend some time collecting evidence and arguments:

▌ Looking back over pages 22–38, find SIX key facts or ideas which support your case.

▌ For each, discuss as a group *how* it supports and 'proves' your argument.

▌ Next, looking back over pages 22–38, find facts or ideas which you suspect your opponents might be going to use to support their case; talk as a group about how you will refute this counter-evidence.

▌ Have the debate, either as a whole class, or as five-minute 'head-to-head' arguments between individuals.

▌ Finally, come together as a whole class to discuss what you have learned from studying this section.

4 Now you are ready to write your report, in three sections:

Start with a sentence:

There is a lot of evidence that life got better, 1509–1745.

Then present the evidence and explain why it gives the impression that the standard of living improved. Say that this was the view of the Whig historians of the late-nineteenth and early-twentieth centuries.

Next, write:

There is, however, a lot of evidence that life did not get better, and in some ways may have got worse.

Then present the evidence and explain why it gives the impression that the standard of living did not improve – or even deteriorated.

Finally, weigh the two opposing interpretations and write a conclusion which explains and justifies where *you* stand in the debate. Explain why it is difficult to come to a firm decision either way.

Why did the ideas of Martin Luther 'go viral'?

4

How did people react to the religious rollercoaster of the English Reformation?

A

← The front cover of Martin Luther's book: *Against the Papacy Founded by the Devil*, written in 1545. It shows the Pope (who has donkey ears) served by demons who are placing the papal crown on his head. He seems unaware that his throne is in the mouth of Hell, and that Hell's flames are burning away its foundations.

Enquiry Step 1: First evidence – asking questions

1 What do you think the artist is telling us about the Pope in picture A?

2 What questions do you have about this?

For hundreds of years, the people of Western Europe followed the ideas of the Catholic Church and the authority of its leader, the Pope. However, in 1517 a German monk named Martin Luther criticised the Catholic Church and – so that people would see his ideas – he nailed them to the door of his local church.

Luther was particularly angry that the Church was selling **indulgences** (which suggested that people could buy forgiveness). Because he was protesting at the Catholic Church, his followers became known as Protestants.

Criticisms of the Catholic Church were nothing new. Luther was influenced by the ideas of the English philosopher John Wycliffe (1320–84), and a Czech priest named Jan Huss (1369–1415).

Wycliffe's ideas had been declared **heresy** and Huss was burned at the stake in 1415.

Unlike Wycliffe or Huss, however, Luther's ideas caught on and spread rapidly across Europe – in today's language, they 'went viral'.

In this way, Luther's small protest led to a much bigger change that historians call the **Reformation**. It split the Catholic Church in two, caused wars, divided countries and even inspired acts of assassination and terrorism.

This section investigates how people reacted to the rollercoaster of religious changes that Luther's protest provoked. For the moment, however, we need to find out what Luther said, and why his ideas spread.

Luther's most important ideas

The only way to gain God's forgiveness and ensure your place in heaven is to believe in Jesus Christ.

Ordinary people do not need priests to help them find God.

The ruler of each country, and not the Pope, should be the leader of their Church.

Believing in Jesus Christ is more important than church ceremonies or going to Mass.

Ordinary people should read the Bible for themselves, in their own language rather than in Latin.

The Church has no need for expensive buildings, ornaments or other treasures.

The wealth of the Church should belong to the ruler of that country.

Priests should be allowed to marry if they choose.

Think

Which of these ideas do you think most concerned the Pope and the Catholic Church? Why do you think this was?

B

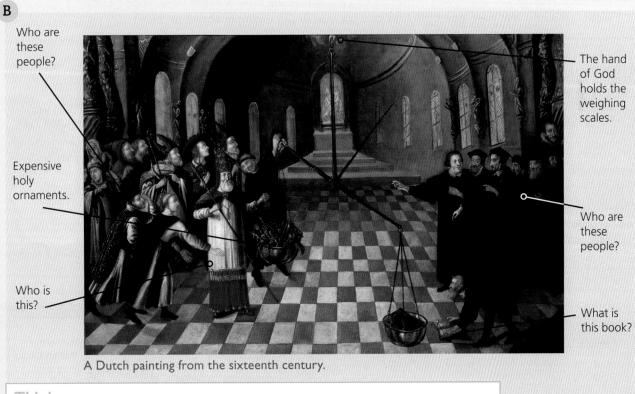

Who are these people?

The hand of God holds the weighing scales.

Expensive holy ornaments.

Who is this?

Who are these people?

What is this book?

A Dutch painting from the sixteenth century.

Think

Try and answer the questions around the picture. Can you work out whether the artist who painted picture B was a Protestant or a Catholic? How can you tell?

4

How did people react to the religious rollercoaster of the English Reformation?

Enquiry Step 2: Suggesting an answer

1 In this enquiry you will investigate why Luther's ideas 'went viral'. Copy each of the headings below onto a separate card. On pages 41–44 you will collect evidence under each of these headings.

| Deals with something that concerns or interests people | Gets noticed by someone 'big' who has influence | Takes advantage of the latest technology | Can be understood by a wide audience | Others 'remix' the idea in some way and pass it on |

2 Working with a partner, carefully read pages 41–43. Using this information, try to suggest as many reasons as you can why Luther's ideas 'went viral' in Germany.

Make a card for each of the reasons you find and place it under one of the heading cards you made. Two examples are provided below (in black). Copy them out and decide which heading each best fits under.

> Many German-speaking people distrusted Italians and were annoyed at how much power the Pope had.
>
> *This meant many German-speaking people were ready to listen to Luther's ideas and were pleased someone was standing up to the Pope.*

> Luther's work was often written in German or translated so that ordinary people could understand his ideas.

3 For each reason you find, add a sentence or two explaining how it might have helped Luther's ideas 'go viral'. We have done the first one for you in the example above (in blue).

Right place? Right time?

Luther lived and worked in Saxony in what today we call Germany. However, in 1517 Germany did not exist. Saxony was just one of many states that made up part of the Holy Roman Empire.

Despite not yet being one country, many people in the Holy Roman Empire spoke German and felt a shared pride in their history. They also had a deep dislike of Italians. This was partly because the Pope was nearly always an Italian and had control over the taxes they paid. The Pope also decided who became bishops in the Holy Roman Empire and almost always chose Italians! When Luther came along, many German-speaking people were proud that one of their own was standing up against the Pope.

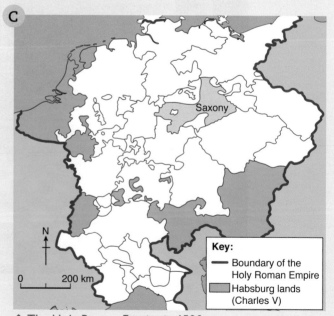

↑ The Holy Roman Empire in 1500.

Key:
— Boundary of the Holy Roman Empire
▨ Habsburg lands (Charles V)

Think

Study Map C. Why might the Holy Roman Emperor Charles V have found it difficult to control ideas in his empire?

Luther's ideas were quickly translated from Latin to German and then copied. In the Middle Ages, books had been copied by hand, which was slow and expensive. However, by the time Luther was writing, printing was well established in most large towns.

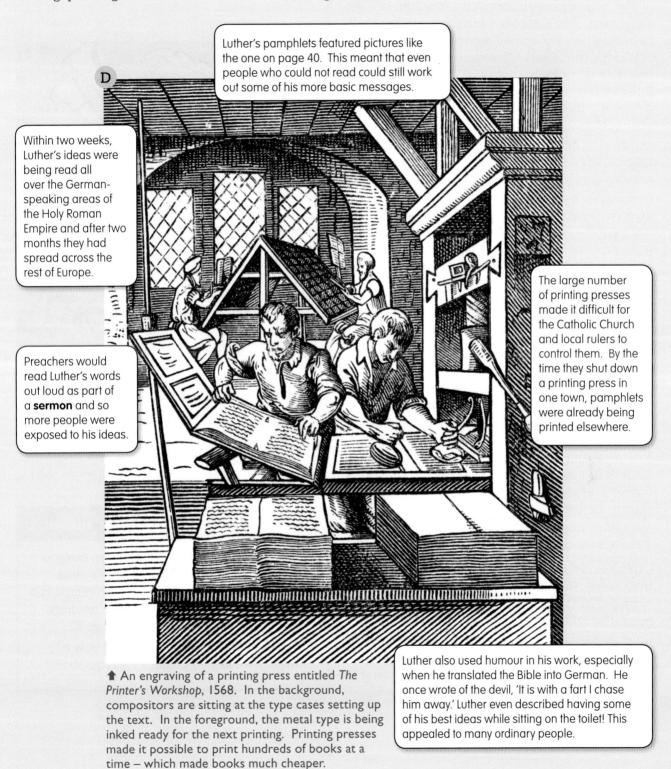

D

Luther's pamphlets featured pictures like the one on page 40. This meant that even people who could not read could still work out some of his more basic messages.

Within two weeks, Luther's ideas were being read all over the German-speaking areas of the Holy Roman Empire and after two months they had spread across the rest of Europe.

The large number of printing presses made it difficult for the Catholic Church and local rulers to control them. By the time they shut down a printing press in one town, pamphlets were already being printed elsewhere.

Preachers would read Luther's words out loud as part of a **sermon** and so more people were exposed to his ideas.

⬆ An engraving of a printing press entitled *The Printer's Workshop*, 1568. In the background, compositors are sitting at the type cases setting up the text. In the foreground, the metal type is being inked ready for the next printing. Printing presses made it possible to print hundreds of books at a time – which made books much cheaper.

Luther also used humour in his work, especially when he translated the Bible into German. He once wrote of the devil, 'It is with a fart I chase him away.' Luther even described having some of his best ideas while sitting on the toilet! This appealed to many ordinary people.

4

How did people react to the religious rollercoaster of the English Reformation?

Rome strikes back

In 1521, the Pope struck back and **excommunicated** Luther, meaning he could no longer attend church services and would not get to Heaven. The Catholic Church wanted Luther to keep quiet, but he had a powerful ally, Frederick the Wise of Saxony. Frederick thought he could increase his own power and independence by protecting Luther. He especially liked Luther's idea that Church wealth should belong to the local ruler. Many other princes in the Holy Roman Empire also began to find Luther's ideas attractive for the same reason.

In the same year that Luther was excommunicated, King Henry VIII of England wrote a book defending the Catholic Church from his criticisms (see page 13). The book became a bestseller across Europe and although it attacked Luther, it gave his ideas more publicity.

Other countries

Once Luther's ideas spread they started to be adapted and developed in different ways. In Switzerland, a **pastor** named Huldrych Zwingli was influenced by Luther's writings, which he used to help develop some of his own ideas. In 1534, after the Pope refused to grant Henry VIII a divorce, the king declared himself Head of the Church in England – an idea he borrowed from Luther's writings for his own purposes! Even though Henry VIII remained a Catholic to his dying day, England was on the way to becoming a Protestant country.

Others said that Luther had not gone far enough. In Geneva, the religious thinker John Calvin argued that the Church needed to be strict and more disciplined to encourage people to live holier lives. He said that church buildings and services needed to be plain so that the congregation was not distracted from listening to the preacher.

E

⬆ Luther shown as the Devil's bagpipes, drawn in 1535.

Enquiry Step 3: Developing your answer

1 Using the information on this page, can you see any more reasons why Luther's ideas 'went viral'? Make a card for each reason you find and place it under one of the headings you made in Enquiry Step 2 on page 42.

2 For each reason you find, explain how it might have helped Luther's ideas 'go viral'.

Enquiry Step 4: Concluding your enquiry

Over the last few pages you discovered a number of reasons why Luther's ideas 'went viral' and spread across Europe. Now it is time to think about which groups of reasons were the most important.

Thinking about importance

One way of thinking about importance is to examine how some groups of reasons might have linked together. Usually the group that links to the most other groups tends to be the most important.

1   Take a sheet of paper and copy the headings you used to sort your reasons under in Enquiry Steps 2 and 3.

2   Draw lines between any of the groups you think might be linked. We have done one link for you in the diagram below. Discuss how these two things might have been linked together.

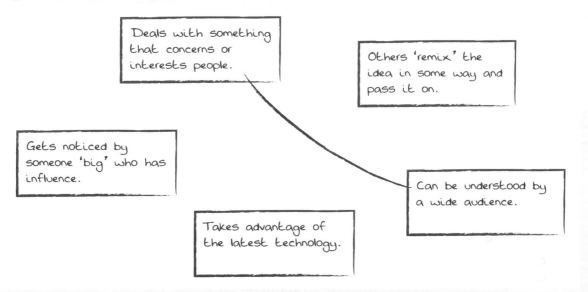

3   Which group of reasons seems to be the most important in explaining why Luther's ideas 'went viral'?

Communicating your answer

You are now ready to attempt an essay that answers the question:

Why did the ideas of Martin Luther 'go viral'?

Your essay should contain the following things:

▌ Introduction – this is where you outline the question and grab the attention of the reader.

▌ Paragraphs – this is the main part of the essay where you examine the reasons that Luther's ideas spread. Each paragraph should describe and explain a group of reasons.

▌ Conclusion – this is where you make a judgement about which reasons you think were the most important and why.

4

How did people react to the religious rollercoaster of the English Reformation?

What can a small church in Devon tell us about religion under the Tudors?

Martin Luther's ideas spread across Europe rapidly and led to years of religious argument. When these Protestant ideas reached England they had an equally powerful effect on the way ordinary people were supposed to worship.

The outside of St Winifred's church in the village of Manaton in Devon looks no different to hundreds of other churches that can be found across the country. Yet step inside and you will see that St Winifred's is home to a beautiful **rood screen**. The rood screen was used to separate the **altar** from the **nave**, where the ordinary people sat. Usually, only the priest was allowed in front of the screen, as this was the holiest part of the Church where he communicated with God during ceremonies such as **Mass**.

Although still beautiful, on closer inspection the rood screen reveals some curious damage. Every single carved and painted figure on the rood screen has had its face deliberately scratched out.

A

⬆ The beautiful rood screen in St Winifred's church. Today, there are only a few such rood screens left in the country. The screen itself was built around 1500 and the yellow parts you can see are decorated with real gold.

In this chapter, you will solve the mystery of what happened to the figures on the St Winifred rood screen and explain when and why this vandalism took place. In doing so you will also find out more about the massive changes to religion that took place under the Tudors.

B

⬆ A group of painted figures on the rood screen.

C

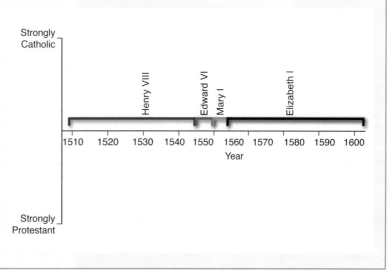

⬆ Close-up of one of the painted figures on the rood screen.

Think

How can you tell that the vandalism shown in pictures B and C was not just some random act committed on the spur of the moment?

Activity

To solve the mystery of rood screen at St Winifred's church we need to understand the religious changes that were affecting the country at the time.

1 Working with a partner or in a small group, read about each of the Tudor monarchs on pages 48–49.

2 Write a short description in a couple of sentences summing up the religious changes each monarch made.

3 Use your descriptions to discuss where to plot the beliefs of each monarch on your own copy of the graph on the right. Look back at the main Protestant ideas on page 41 to help you.

4 Join the points up on your graph. Why do you think the Tudor period has sometimes been described as a religious 'rollercoaster'?

Strongly Catholic — Henry VIII, Edward VI, Mary I, Elizabeth I — 1510 1520 1530 1540 1550 1560 1570 1580 1590 1600 Year — Strongly Protestant

Henry VIII (1509–47)

- In 1521, Henry VIII wrote a book defending the Catholic faith and attacking Protestant ideas. He was awarded the title 'Defender of the Faith.'
- In 1534, Henry VIII broke with Rome and made himself Head of the Church in England. This was so he could divorce Catherine of Aragon and marry Anne Boleyn. He remained, however, a Catholic.
- In 1536–40, Henry dissolved the Catholic monasteries so he could take control of their land and wealth.
- In 1539, Henry passed measures known as the Six Articles. These protected six key Catholic ideas. Protestants called the law 'the whip with six strings' because they were severely punished if they did not accept it.
- In 1540, Henry had the Bible translated from Latin into English so that everyone could understand it.

Edward VI (1547–53)

- Edward was brought up as a Protestant and, like his father, was regarded as Head of the Church in England.
- In 1548, a law was passed saying priests had to wear plain robes rather than the old brightly coloured ones. Also, they were allowed to get married for the first time.
- Pictures on church walls were whitewashed. Statues of saints were removed as they were seen as Catholic superstition and stopped people having a more direct relationship with God.
- Ornaments such as golden goblets and candlesticks were sold. Many stained glass windows were smashed as they were seen as a distraction from the words of the preacher.
- Some Catholic Bishops were imprisoned in the Tower of London.
- In 1549, a new Prayer Book was introduced. It was written in English and not Latin so that everyone could understand it.
- In 1552 the Catholic Mass was abolished and was replaced with a much simpler Protestant 'communion' service. Stone altars were replaced with plain wooden tables.

Mary I (1553–58)

- Mary released the Catholic bishops who had been locked in the Tower of London. Protestant leaders were imprisoned instead.
- In 1554, Mary married Prince Philip. He was heir to the Spanish throne and a devout Catholic.
- In 1554, the country was officially reunited with the Catholic Church. The Pope was declared Head of the Church.
- Married priests were expelled from the Church.
- Latin Church services and Latin Bibles were brought back. The English Prayer book was banned.
- Between 1555 and 1558, around 300 Protestants were burned to death for refusing to accept Catholic beliefs.

Elizabeth I (1558–1603)

Elizabeth was raised a Protestant but tried to find a 'Middle Way' in religion, introducing the 'Thirty-Nine Articles' in 1563.

- Elizabeth called herself Governor, and not Head of the Church.
- Elizabeth brought back the English Prayer Book and church services were conducted in English rather than Latin.
- Priests could once again get married if they wished.
- Priests were allowed to wear brightly coloured robes and church services did not have to be simple.
- Some lines attacking the Pope were removed from the Prayer Book.

In 1570, however, the Pope excommunicated Elizabeth – after this, she faced a number of Catholic plots. Therefore, Catholic priests were hunted down, tortured and executed.

4

How did people react to the religious rollercoaster of the English Reformation?

How 'bloody' was Queen Mary?

On a rainy day in London, a large crowd had gathered. They watched as the white bearded old man carefully climbed the scaffold and began to speak. He declared that the Pope was the Antichrist and that the Protestant religion was the true faith, before being pulled down by the guards. Next he was led to a stake, around which bundles of wood had been carefully arranged. With a cheerful expression on his face, he threw off his shirt and went to his death.

A

⬆ A Protestant woodcut of the execution of Archbishop Cranmer in 1556. Cranmer had been Archbishop of Canterbury during the reigns of Henry VIII and Edward VI. When Mary became Queen in 1553, he was arrested and put on trial for treason. He was forced to sign a public notice saying he had been wrong in his Protestant beliefs. He was then sentenced to death by burning.

Think

Before the flames consumed him, eyewitnesses saw Cranmer plunge his right hand into the fire and shout, 'This is the hand that hath offended.' Why do you think he did this?

You have already seen that religion was a hot topic during Tudor times. On pages 48–49 you saw how different rulers made changes to the Church and the way people were supposed to worship God. Cranmer had been one of King Henry's most trusted religious advisers but ended up accused of heresy. It was clear that Queen Mary was determined to bring back Catholicism to England.

The traditional view of Queen Mary is as a cruel and wicked monarch. She has featured in the *Horrible Histories* series of books and television programmes and usually gets a very negative press! It is no coincidence that most people know her as 'bloody' Mary.

In this chapter you will focus on evaluating the reputation of Queen Mary (1553–58) and decide whether she deserves such a negative reputation and nickname.

Evidence against Mary

Activity

1 Extract B sums up the main arguments for Mary's negative and 'bloody' reputation. These are outlined in the first column of the table below.

Charges against Mary	Evidence that supports the charge	Evidence that refutes the charge
Mary was stubborn and unusually cruel		
People at the time were horrified by Mary's actions and the number of burnings		
Mary's actions were pointless as the country was mainly Protestant. The burnings changed nothing.		

2 Use the information on pages 50–51 to find evidence that supports the three different charges and fill in the second column of your table. Add a sentence explaining how the evidence supports each charge.

B

The Protestants would not give up their religion. They were burned alive ... In three years nearly three hundred people were put to death by Mary's cruel orders. Yet she did no good but rather harm to her cause. For many who were at first on her side turned away with horror from her dreadful cruelties.

An extract from the book, *Our Island Story*, by H.E. Marshall, 1905.

C

The Tudors and heretics

- Henry VII burned 10 in 24 years.
- Henry VIII burned 81 in 38 years.
- Edward VI burned 2 in 6 years.
- Mary burned 284 in 5 years.
- Elizabeth burned 5 in 45 years.

D

Some of the onlookers wept, others prayed to God to give him strength to bear the pain, others gathered the ashes and bones and wrapped them in paper to preserve them, others threatened the bishops. I think it would be wise not to be too firm against Protestants, otherwise I forsee that the people may cause a revolt.

The Spanish Ambassador writing in 1555, describing the first Protestant being burnt at the stake.

E

Mary did not seem to regret sending so many people to the flames. She continued signing orders for executions, even up until the day that she died.

F

Although Mary ordered the execution of several well-known and important Protestants such as Archbishop Cranmer, the majority of those who were burnt were ordinary people like weavers and labourers.

Think

The description in extract D was written by the Spanish Ambassador who was a Catholic. Do you think we can trust his account? Explain your thinking.

4

How did people react to the religious rollercoaster of the English Reformation?

Evidence in support of Mary

Not all historians agree with the traditional view of 'bloody' Queen Mary. The information on pages 52–53 could be used to **refute** (disprove) some of the charges against her.

G Mary's father-in-law Charles V of Spain ordered more than 30,000 Protestants to be put to death in Europe. They were burnt, hanged and even buried alive.

I During the 1500s punishments were extremely harsh and people could be hanged for small offences such as minor theft. Public executions were common and often drew very large crowds of spectators.

J People widely accepted that the punishment for heresy should be burning. This had gone on since the Middle Ages. Both Protestants and Catholics accepted this.

H

⬆ The front cover of Foxe's *Book of Martyrs*, published in 1563. Nearly all our evidence about the burnings comes from this one source. Foxe was a clergyman during the reign of Elizabeth and was very one-sided in his beliefs. He was writing to praise Protestantism and to show how evil Mary was so that people would turn away from Catholicism. He also wanted to show how bad things had been under Mary so people would feel more positive towards Queen Elizabeth who was not yet secure on the throne when the book was published.

Activity

3 Working with a partner or in a small group, look at the evidence on pages 52–53 and discuss how each example might be used to refute the charges against Mary.

4 Fill in the final column of your table and make sure you write a sentence or two explaining how the evidence refutes the charge against Mary.

5 Decide what the 'clinching' or strongest argument is. In other words, if you could only use one piece of evidence to challenge or prove Mary's negative reputation, which one would you use?

K

Some modern historians argue that the burnings had the desired effect. They were meant to deter Protestants and by the end of Mary's reign there was a gradual fall in the numbers of those accused of heresy.

L

Mary changed the law to make churches look more Catholic. Many parishes enthusiastically began this process even before the law was passed. Records show that most parishes decorated their churches more than the legal minimum required.

M

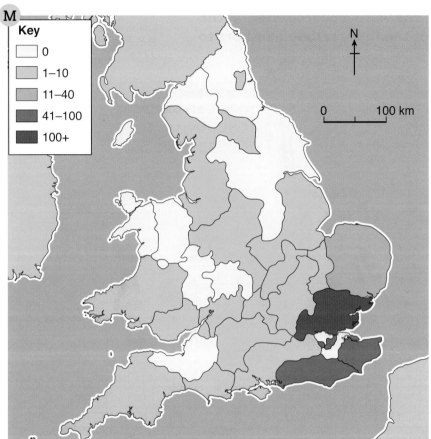

Key
- 0
- 1–10
- 11–40
- 41–100
- 100+

N

0 ——— 100 km

⬆ Numbers of Protestants burned by region during Mary's reign.

Think

Look at map M. What pattern do you notice in where the burnings took place? Do you think there was strong Protestant belief in all parts of the country? Explain why.

Activity

6 Discuss as a class where you stand on the issue of Mary's reputation. Be prepared to share your reasons with the rest of the class.

7 Now it is time to write up your evaluation of Mary and answer the question:

How 'bloody' was Queen Mary?

An evaluation must consider both sides of the argument before reaching a decision. You may like to use the ideas below to help you structure your work:

▌ Introduction – this should grab the attention of the reader with an interesting fact about Mary and her reputation. It should also briefly outline the question you are answering.

▌ Main paragraphs – deal with each of the charges against Mary in a separate paragraph. Firstly, outline the charge (you can use the first column in your table). Next, provide evidence that supports it before giving evidence that refutes it. Finally, end each paragraph with a sentence explaining what YOU think – was Mary guilty of that particular charge?

▌ Conclusion – this is where you decide overall whether Mary deserves her negative reputation and nickname. You could save your 'clinching' argument for this final part of the essay.

4

How did people react to the religious rollercoaster of the English Reformation?

How did the Tudor religious 'rollercoaster' affect ordinary people?

You have already read on pages 48–49 how the Tudor monarchs kept changing the official religion of the country. By now you can see why we decided to use the word 'rollercoaster' in the section title. In fact, we are not the first textbook authors to use that analogy!

⬇ Religious rollercoaster adapted from a diagram in Peter Moss, *History Alive 1485–1714* (1968).

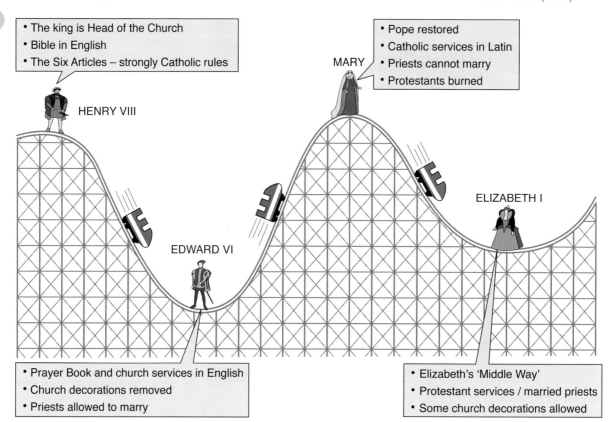

A

• The king is Head of the Church
• Bible in English
• The Six Articles – strongly Catholic rules

HENRY VIII

MARY

• Pope restored
• Catholic services in Latin
• Priests cannot marry
• Protestants burned

ELIZABETH I

EDWARD VI

• Prayer Book and church services in English
• Church decorations removed
• Priests allowed to marry

• Elizabeth's 'Middle Way'
• Protestant services / married priests
• Some church decorations allowed

But how did these changes affect ordinary people – did their beliefs change backwards and forwards as the laws changed? Their voices have remained silent as most of them were **illiterate** and have left no first-hand testimony. So what exactly did they believe and how did they 'ride' the Tudor religious rollercoaster? Historians disagree about how ordinary people reacted to the religious changes under the Tudors.

Most ordinary people disliked Catholicism even before they were told to. They became enthusiastic Protestants as soon as it was on offer. The Catholic Church was a rotten structure – it just needed a kick to knock it down and it never recovered after Edward!

⬆ The traditional Whig view

I disagree! The majority of people had a lasting fondness for Catholicism, even long after Elizabeth had come to the throne. It was an important part of their lives and they were in no hurry to let go of it.

⬆ The revisionist view

Evidence from parish records

If you look back to pages 48–49 you will see how Edward, Mary and then Elizabeth all gave orders changing how church services were conducted and even the way that churches looked on the inside. Therefore, parish records provide clues about how ordinary communities responded to these changes.

All historians would want you to be careful about the way you interpret this information:

EVIDENCE ALERT!

- Tudor government was well-organised and made effective use of visitations (inspections) to make sure religious changes were being carried out around the country.
- Inspectors confiscated property and money from local churches that were too slow to make changes.
- The decisions made by priests and churchwardens may not always have reflected the opinions of everyone in their parish.

Evidence from Edward VI's reign, 1547–53

B

Ashburton Church in Devon, 1547–48
- 2s 4d for taking down an image of Saint George.
- 3s 4d for removal of the rood screen and other images.

Tilney Church in Norfolk, 1547
- 35s paid out for whiting [whitewashing] of the church and stopping [filling] of the holes (where statues and images had been).

Melford Church in Suffolk, 1547–48
- 7s 1d paid for taking down of images.
- 1s 2d paid for taking down of the font and high altar.
- £1 14s 8d paid for whitewashing of the church.

A selection of parish records from across the country.

Activity

Working with a partner, look at evidence B–G in turn.
1 For each decide whether it suggests that people willingly embraced Protestantism, or that they clung onto Catholic beliefs.
2 Why do you think so many places changed to Protestantism without resistance?

C

In 1549, there was a Prayer Book Rebellion in Cornwall and Devon – 7000 armed men rose against Edward VI's religious changes. The royal army massacred them.

D

Hundreds of images, statues and **vestments** were hidden during Edward's reign. At Morebath in Devon, the colourful vestments worn by the priest were handed out among the community for safekeeping. In other places statues, ornaments and images were buried or even walled in to prevent them being found by government inspectors.

E

The majority of parish records reveal that by the end of Edward's reign the altars were almost all gone, as were the images and statues. Many of these items were sold off. The great majority of churches had done as they were ordered.

F

Even before Edward changed the law in 1548, there were a few attacks by gangs on statues and other images. These were mainly in London and the south east of England.

G

Between 1547 and 1549, the printing of Protestant pamphlets and books increased a great deal. There must have been a demand for such works for printers to go to the expense of printing them.

4

How did people react to the religious rollercoaster of the English Reformation?

Evidence from Mary's reign, 1553–58

H

The historian Ronald Hutton examined 134 parish records and discovered the following about churches during Mary's reign:

- By the end of 1554, all had replaced their high altars and recovered the colourful vestments worn by Catholic priests.
- Most churches were more decorated than the minimum required by the law.
- By the end of Mary's reign in 1558, most churches had restored their rood screens.

I

Many images, statues and other goods sold off under Edward were returned cheaply or loaned back to churches as soon as Mary became queen.

J

Mary faced resistance, and 284 Protestants were burned during her reign. Most of these were ordinary people – weavers, cloth workers and labourers who decided to perish in the flames rather than change their beliefs.

Evidence from Elizabeth's reign, 1558–1603

K

During Elizabeth's reign the removal of altars and decoration was ordered. However, four years later a survey showed only half the churches in Lincolnshire had got rid of their altars as instructed. Furthermore, 82 parishes delayed the destruction of images, books and vestments for three or more years.

L

'The villagers weep and bewail seeing the bare walls, and lacking their images and chalices.'

From an Elizabethan report on Weaverham in Cheshire, 1589.

Activity

3 Working with a partner, look at evidence H–J, then K–L in turn. For each piece of evidence decide whether it suggests people clung on to their existing beliefs, or that they willingly embraced Catholicism/Protestantism.

4 Working as a whole class, based on your studies of evidence B–L, decide whether you 'agree strongly', 'agree', 'disagree' or 'disagree strongly' with the following statements:

▌ The majority of parish churches acted quickly to make the changes ordered during the reigns of Edward, Mary and Elizabeth.

▌ Edward's laws met with little resistance and so the population must have already been Protestant in their beliefs.

▌ There was little appetite for Catholicism by the time Mary came to the throne, even though she made laws to restore it.

▌ Some ordinary Elizabethan people still clung to aspects of Catholic belief.

5 Explain your reasons for each decision using the information you have studied.

The evidence from wills

What a parish church decides to do, or not to do, does not necessarily tell us what was going on in people's hearts. For this reason, historians have made much use of the wills left by ordinary Tudor people to try to shed light on their personal beliefs. Catholics believed in the saints and the Virgin Mary but Protestants believed this was superstition. Therefore, a will which mentions the saints and the Virgin Mary suggests a person of Catholic belief, whereas a will which asks Jesus Christ for salvation suggests a Protestant faith.

M

Reign	Durham and York	Hull	Canterbury	London
Edward VI	8	Not known	8	32
Mary	6	4	8	20
Elizabeth I	31	49	Not known	Not known

⬆ Percentage of wills with Protestant introductions.

All historians would want you to be careful about the way you interpret Tudor wills:

* Many people could not read or write, and asked their local priest to write their will for them – so the words may not represent what they personally believed.
* In Tudor society the rule of law and loyalty to the monarch were taken very seriously by most people.
* Mary's government passed heresy laws, which meant that those who refused to accept Catholicism could be burned. In contrast, no one was executed for heresy when Edward was king.

Activity

6 Working as a whole class, study table M, and decide whether you 'agree strongly', 'agree', 'disagree' or 'disagree strongly' with the following statements:
   ▮ The way wills were written kept changing under the Tudor monarchs.
   ▮ Most people had become Protestant by the end of Edward VI's reign.
   ▮ Mary had great success in turning people's beliefs back to Catholicism.
   ▮ Some ordinary Elizabethan people still clung to aspects of Catholic belief.

7 Explain your reasons for each decision using the information you have studied.

8 Looking back at page 54 to remind yourselves of the 'traditional' and 'revisionist' views of how ordinary people responded to the Tudor religious 'rollercoaster':
   ▮ Which interpretation do you most agree with? Explain your reasons using facts and arguments.
   OR
   ▮ Suggest your own interpretation, explaining your reasons using facts and arguments.

9 Finally, what factors make the task of the historian trying to find out about ordinary people's beliefs so difficult?

4

How did people react to the religious rollercoaster of the English Reformation?

Gunpowder, treason and plot – what was the government up to in 1605?

Every year on 5 November we celebrate a failed terrorist attack that dates back over 400 years. Yet how much do you really know about the events of 1605 and the plot to blow up King James I and Parliament? In this section we have already examined the great religious changes rulers made. But what lengths were people willing to go to, in order to defend their religious beliefs?

James I became king in 1603. Many Catholics were hopeful that he would let them worship more freely. There had been some encouraging signs and King James himself was even married to a Catholic. However, the members of James' council and many MPs were strongly Protestant. They believed that the country would be weakened if Catholics were given any more freedom.

Therefore, in 1604, James declared his, 'utter detestation' of Catholics! The laws against them were tightened and became even harsher. Although disappointed, most Catholics accepted the changes. However, a few determined gentlemen had other ideas.

⬇ The story of the Gunpowder Plot.

Robert Catesby hatched a plan to blow up Parliament, kill the king and put a Catholic monarch on the throne.

One of the plotters, Guy Fawkes, filled a vault underneath the Houses of Parliament with 36 barrels of gunpowder, more than enough to destroy Parliament and everyone in it.

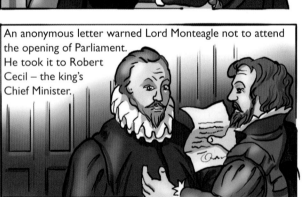

An anonymous letter warned Lord Monteagle not to attend the opening of Parliament. He took it to Robert Cecil – the king's Chief Minister.

The vaults underneath Parliament were searched and Guy Fawkes was arrested. He was tortured to make him reveal the names of the other plotters and sign a confession.

The rest of the plotters escaped. However, 200 soldiers caught up with them at Holbeach House. Catesby and a number of other plotters were killed in the fighting. The others were brought back to London for trial.

A

⬆ A print from 1605, showing the gunpowder plotters' execution. They were dragged through the crowded streets on **hurdles** before being hanged. They were then **disembowelled** and their bodies quartered. Finally, their heads were put on spikes outside the House of Lords.

Think

Why do you think the plotters were publicly executed in such a gruesome way?

Activity

I Many historians believe there is more to the Gunpowder Plot than first meets the eye. Some have even gone as far as to say that the government knew about the plot or even set the whole thing up to make Catholics look bad. This would have given them an excuse to crack down on Catholics even further. Others insist that the plot was simply an ambitious plan that went wrong. Based only on the evidence you have looked at so far, where do you stand on the debate?

How involved was the government?

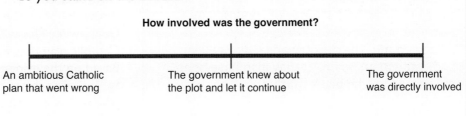

An ambitious Catholic plan that went wrong

The government knew about the plot and let it continue

The government was directly involved

How did people react to the religious rollercoaster of the English Reformation?

4

Some curious facts

Historians must consider a range of evidence before reaching a conclusion. Read the information on this page carefully and discuss what it might suggest.

B

My lord, I have care for your safety. Therefore, I would advise you devise some excuse to miss your attendance at this Parliament. For God and man have come together to punish the wickedness of this time. Go into the country, for they shall receive a terrible blow this Parliament – and yet they shall not see who hurts them.

Part of the letter sent to Lord Monteagle. We cannot be sure who sent the letter but we do know that one of the plotters, Francis Tresham, was brother-in-law to Lord Monteagle.

C

After receiving the warning letter, Lord Monteagle took it immediately to Robert Cecil – King James' First Minister. The king had been hunting but saw the letter on his return to London on 31 October. Yet the government took no action until 4 November.

D

When the plotters were tracked down at Holbeach House, Catesby was shot dead in the fighting. The soldier who shot him was awarded a generous pension by the government even though Catesby would have been a useful prisoner to question.

E

At the time of the plot, the government controlled gunpowder supplies. The biggest store was kept in the Tower of London. However, gunpowder may have been smuggled into the country and Guy Fawkes had contacts in Spain. It may also have been purchased on the **black market**.

Think

Does letter B give enough information for the government:
- to realise there was a plot?
- to realise that the plot was to use gunpowder to blow up Parliament?
- to search the vaults under Parliament?

F

The plotters were tipped off that a letter had been sent to Lord Monteagle. However, they decided to continue with the plan.

G

Before the plot, Robert Cecil told the Venetian Ambassador that he thought the king had been too kind to Catholics, and that James' life was in danger. Cecil wanted to expose and destroy the Catholics.

H

The government had a well-developed network of spies. Guy Fawkes had visited Flanders hoping to get foreign support for the plot but was spotted by English spies. They reported back to Robert Cecil and linked Fawkes to Catesby, who had been involved in earlier plots.

Activity

2 How does each of these 'curious facts' (B–H) throw doubt on the theory that the Gunpowder Plot was simply an ambitious Catholic plan that went wrong?
3 Based on the evidence you have looked at so far, including the curious facts on this page, where now do you stand on the debate about how involved the government was in the Plot?
4 If you have changed your position, discuss your reasons for doing so. Which information made you change your mind and why?

The after-effects of the plot

On 5 November 1605, church bells were rung and bonfires lit to celebrate the discovery of the plot. The government ordered that this become an annual event to celebrate the king's heaven-sent deliverance from the 'evil' Catholic plotters.

The government also printed the 'King's Book' – containing James' own account of what happened. It contained the confession of Guy Fawkes and added to the public's feelings of shock and horror.

King James argued that the majority of Catholics were loyal. However, in 1606 he supported new laws that increased restrictions on their freedom of worship. In the years that followed the plot, other laws were passed preventing Catholics from being lawyers, serving as officers in the army or navy, or voting in elections.

⬆ Do we burn the right 'guy' every 5 November?

After the gunpowder plot, there were no more Catholic plots in England, Wales or Scotland. It seemed like the Catholic threat was over and the country was more firmly Protestant than ever before. However, Protestant suspicions continued and life for Catholics remained uncomfortable. When the Great Fire of London broke out in 1666, Londoners were (wrongly) quick to point the finger of blame at Catholics!

Think

Who stood to gain from the discovery of a Catholic plot?

Activity

5 After considering the effects of the Gunpowder Plot along with the earlier evidence, it is time to make your mind up about where you stand on the debate about how involved the government was in the Plot. Be prepared to explain the reasons for your position.

How involved was the government?

An ambitious Catholic plan that went wrong | The government knew about the plot and let it continue | The government was directly involved

6 Why is it so difficult for historians to be sure about whether the government knew about or was involved in the plot?
7 Some historians believe that England 'became a fully Protestant country' only in 1605.
▍ What evidence on pages 58–61 supports this idea?
▍ What evidence would you produce to contradict this interpretation?

Did religious toleration benefit everyone, 1603–1745?

You have already seen how religion could be a dangerous issue under the Tudors. The Stuart period could have ended with a bang was it not for the discovery of the Gunpowder Plot, and having the wrong religious beliefs could still get you killed. In 1612, King James ordered the burning of Edward Wightman as a heretic. He had denied the resurrection of Jesus Christ and declared himself appointed by God to save the world. This was the last execution for heresy in England. By 1689, many different religious beliefs had sprung up around the country and were tolerated under the law. So what was different, and did everyone benefit from the changing attitudes?

1604 Hampton Court Conference

King James I tightened laws against Catholics. Extreme Protestants, known as Puritans, were disappointed when James failed to listen to their recommendations for the Church. A new translation of the Bible was ordered – this 'King James' version is still in use today.

1605 The Gunpowder Plot

A plot to blow up King James and replace him with a Catholic ruler was prevented (see pages 58–61). After the plot, laws against Catholics became even harsher.

1620 The Mayflower sets sail

Puritans searching for a better life and more religious freedom set sail for America to establish their own colonies. Those Puritans remaining continued to believe that the Church of England should go further and be much stricter.

1635 Laud is made Archbishop of Canterbury

Archbishop Laud wanted church services to be more ceremonial and churches to be decorated with stained glass and other ornaments. Many accused him of being too Catholic in his ideas. He ordered a crackdown on Puritan preachers. One preacher, William Prynne, had his ears 'cropped' as a punishment.

1649 The 'World Turned Upside Down'

After the execution of King Charles, many people felt freer to think and speak, as they liked. Some believed that the end of the world was coming, so organised religion was no longer needed. Different religious groups such as the Quakers and the Fifth Monarchists emerged with radical new ideas (see page 89).

1653–60 The Protectorate

The Puritans became the most powerful religious group. People were encouraged to work hard, eat ordinary food and wear plain clothes. Many inns were shut and theatres were closed. Most sports were banned. People could even be fined for swearing.

1661–65 The Clarendon Code

Laws were made that banned Catholics from holding public office. A new Book of Common Prayer was introduced and became compulsory in churches. It remained unchanged for over 300 years. Those who did not follow the Book of Common Prayer were labelled **Nonconformists** and banned from worshipping in groups of more than four.

1701 The Act of Settlement

Parliament made a law that no Roman Catholic, nor anyone married to a Roman Catholic, could hold the English Crown. This remains the case today.

1687–1688 Declaration of Indulgence

It was well known that King James II was a Catholic. He ordered a declaration giving Catholics freedom to worship openly. Parliament was furious. Six bishops refused to read the declaration out in church. They were put on trial and found not guilty – a humiliation for the king.

1689 Toleration Act

Nonconformists were given more freedom to worship. Catholics were given no extra freedoms.

1715 Jacobite Rebellion

In 1715, the Catholic James Edward Stuart (son of James II) led an unsuccessful rebellion against George I. Many Scots thought they could break free of England if the Stuart monarchy returned.

1745 Second Jacobite Rebellion

Charles Stuart (grandson of James II), also known as Bonnie Prince Charlie, led a second attempt at reclaiming the throne for his family. His forces were smashed at the Battle of Culloden in 1746.

1688 The Glorious Revolution

After James II had a son, Parliament feared a Catholic succession and so invited James' Protestant daughter and her husband William of Orange to rule. King James fled to France when it became clear he had few supporters. Parliament made William and Mary agree to a Bill of Rights (see page 92) which specified that only a Protestant could inherit the crown.

Activity

Read through the events on pages 62–63 and use them to help you answer questions 1–3.

1. At what point was it too late for Catholicism to make a comeback as the official religion? Explain your thinking.
2. Who seemed to have more control over religion in this period, the monarchy or Parliament?
3. Did everyone benefit from more tolerant religious attitudes 1603–1745? Put the following groups in order to show who gained the most in the period. Add a sentence to each explaining your choice:
   - Moderate Protestants
   - Catholics
   - Nonconformists
   - Puritans.
4. The next book in this series looks at the period 1745–1901, when Britain underwent massive changes. Scientific advances led to an industrial revolution that changed the way people worked and lived and Britain further expanded its Empire. What do you predict happened to religion in this period?

5

What can Lucy Hay tell us about life during the English Civil War?

What can Lucy Hay tell us about life during the English Civil War?

The life of Lucy Hay

Historians debate whether individual people can change the times in which they live – or whether we are all just swept along by forces out of our control. This section focuses on the life of one woman, Lucy Hay. She lived through one of the dynamic and unsettled periods in our history, the time of civil war.

When Lucy Hay first went to the royal **court** in 1614, the seeds of the **Civil War** were already sown.

The confrontation between the king and Parliament was mainly about money. Rapidly rising prices during the reign of King James I (1603–25) had all-but-bankrupted the monarchy. But, when James' son, Charles I (1625–49) asked for more taxes, he found himself refused by a Parliament which was demanding more influence, trying to interfere in the Church of England, and telling him which countries he ought to be going to war with.

It was a recipe for disaster. Charles I believed in **Divine Right** – that he was appointed king by God and should be obeyed. Charles tried to rule without Parliament. But when war broke out with Scotland in 1639, the king was trapped – he could not afford the war, and was forced to call Parliament.

After Parliament was recalled, relations between King and Parliament rapidly descended into Civil War. Charles I was executed in 1649 (see pages 2–3) and for eleven years England was governed without a king; this period is called 'the **Interregnum**' (a Latin word meaning 'between reigns').

Throughout this period of conflict and chaotic change lived our heroine – Lucy Hay. In this section, you are going to study the Civil War through her eyes and experiences. You will consider what her life story tells us about life during the wars. And you will be asked to decide whether she influenced events … or whether she was merely influenced by them.

Prepare to be amazed!

Activity

1 The diagram on page 65 shows the events of the reign of Charles I. Study and discuss them with a partner or in a small group to choose:
  ▮ THREE events which would have outraged Parliament. Explain why.
  ▮ THREE events which would have outraged Charles I. Again, explain why.
2 In fact, all ten events 1625–42 helped to cause the Civil War. Sort them into the three different categories – 'Conflicts about religion', 'Conflicts about money' and 'Conflicts about Divine Right'.
3 Coming together as a whole class, share your findings. What, in your opinion, was the chief cause of the Civil War?

Relations between king and Parliament spiralling out of control

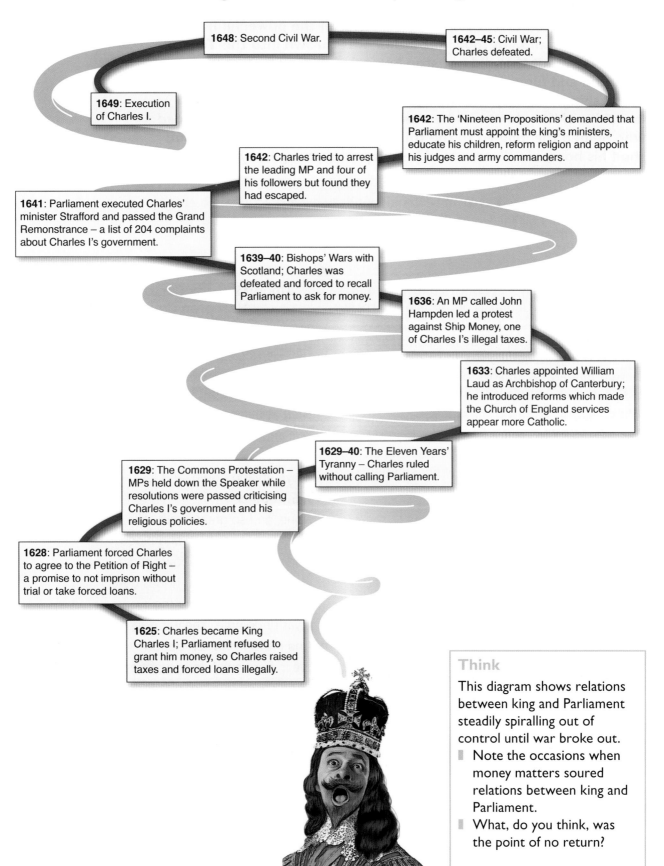

1648: Second Civil War.

1642–45: Civil War; Charles defeated.

1649: Execution of Charles I.

1642: The 'Nineteen Propositions' demanded that Parliament must appoint the king's ministers, educate his children, reform religion and appoint his judges and army commanders.

1642: Charles tried to arrest the leading MP and four of his followers but found they had escaped.

1641: Parliament executed Charles' minister Strafford and passed the Grand Remonstrance – a list of 204 complaints about Charles I's government.

1639–40: Bishops' Wars with Scotland; Charles was defeated and forced to recall Parliament to ask for money.

1636: An MP called John Hampden led a protest against Ship Money, one of Charles I's illegal taxes.

1633: Charles appointed William Laud as Archbishop of Canterbury; he introduced reforms which made the Church of England services appear more Catholic.

1629–40: The Eleven Years' Tyranny – Charles ruled without calling Parliament.

1629: The Commons Protestation – MPs held down the Speaker while resolutions were passed criticising Charles I's government and his religious policies.

1628: Parliament forced Charles to agree to the Petition of Right – a promise to not imprison without trial or take forced loans.

1625: Charles became King Charles I; Parliament refused to grant him money, so Charles raised taxes and forced loans illegally.

Think

This diagram shows relations between king and Parliament steadily spiralling out of control until war broke out.

▍ Note the occasions when money matters soured relations between king and Parliament.

▍ What, do you think, was the point of no return?

5

What can Lucy Hay tell us about life during the English Civil War?

Who was Lucy Hay?

Lucy Percy was born in 1599, the daughter of the powerful Earl of Northumberland. In 1606, her father was thrown into the Tower for treason, but that did not stop her going to Court. She was beautiful and fun and, sometime after 1614, she caught the eye of the dashing, recently widowed James Hay. James Hay was a favourite of King James I – he was the Groom of the Stool (the lord who helped the king go to the toilet). He threw lavish parties and shod his horses in silver … and he swept the young Lucy off her feet!

Lucy's father tried to stop her by keeping her with him in the Tower, but in 1617 she escaped. James was away in Scotland, but he knew how to wow a teenage girl – he gave her £2000 (worth £314,000 today) to spend on parties until he returned.

Mrs Hay

Lucy and James Hay were married in 1617, and Lucy became the 'Countess of Carlisle'. In those dangerous days, women's lives were not easy. She had a son in 1618, but he lived only for a month; four years later she almost died of an illness that left her unable to have children, and in 1628 she fell seriously ill with **smallpox**.

Even so, she became a favourite at Court. She was a serious flirt, and it was rumoured that, to help her husband's career, she was having an affair with the powerful Duke of Buckingham.

The queen's favourite

Charles became king in 1625. The new queen, Henrietta Maria, was French and Catholic and very prim and proper, and at first she did not like Lucy, finding her too racy and intimidating. But, by inviting the Queen to her women-only parties – the latest exciting fashion from France – Lucy quickly became the Queen's favourite.

By the 1630s, Lucy had grown into a strong woman who knew her own mind. She was tired of the fashions and dances of the court, and of having no real power of her own.

So Lucy tried another idea from France: the **salon** – where rich older women would entertain and talk politics with eager young **courtiers**. They loved her because she could get them noticed at court … and she became an influential person in her own right about whom young men wrote gushing poems.

A

Upon My Lady Carlisle's Walking In Hampton Court Garden

Thomas says:

Heardst thou not music when she talked?
And didst not find that as she walked
She threw rare perfumes all about,
Such as bean-blossoms newly out …
Dull and insensible, couldst thou not see
A thing so near a **deity**
Move up and down, and feel no change?

J. S. replies

None, and so great, were alike strange;
Alas! Tom, I am flesh and blood,
And was consulting how I could
In spite of masks and hoods descry
The parts denied unto the eye.
I was undoing all she wore,
And had she walked but one turn more,
Eve in her first state had not been
More naked or more plainly seen.

Thomas says:

'Twas well for thee she left the place;
There is great danger in that face.

Many poets wrote poems lavishing praise on Lucy. In this rude parody, the poet and courtier John Suckling mocked his friend Thomas Carew's gushing flattery.

B

One of the features of the royal court in the seventeenth century were masques – lavish theatrical productions, in which the royal family and nobles starred. This painting by the Dutch artist Gerrit van Honthorst shows a masque held by the Duke of Buckingham in 1628. Can you spot the following in the picture?

- King Charles, dressed as Apollo the sun god, and Queen Henrietta Maria as Diana the goddess of chastity (you can see her holding Diana's hunting bow).
- Charles and Henrietta Maria, with her ladies-in-waiting, descending from heaven on a moving platform.
- Hate and Envy being cast into hell by Love and Goodness.
- The scapegoat – a religious symbol, carrying all the sins of the nation into hell.
- The Duke of Buckingham, dressed as Mercury the gods' messenger, presenting the king and queen with all the blessings of culture and learning.
- Lucy Hay (top left), whispering in the Queen's ear – why is this so very significant?

Activity

1 Read out loud, and discuss as a whole class, poem A opposite. Why is it so funny? What do the last two lines mean?
2 Discuss in a small group, then share as a class, what pages 66–67 tell us about:

Lucy Hay	Seventeenth-century women	Politics at the court of Charles I

(Copy this table and use it to record your thoughts.)

3 Start a 'Timeline of events in the life of Lucy Hay'. List on it the more important events you have learned about so far.
4 At this period of her life, Lucy Hay was very successful. Was she merely taking advantage of events as they happened, or was she affecting events and 'making history' herself?

5

What can Lucy Hay tell us about life during the English Civil War?

Lucy and the outbreak of civil war

James Hay died in 1636. Lucy was at the peak of her fame and celebrity ... but, in a world where women influenced events only through their husbands, James' death could have been a terrifying setback.

King versus Parliament

Lucy's was not the only world falling apart in the 1630s. In 1628, King Charles had quarrelled with his Parliament, which had forced him to sign their **Petition of Right**. He had dissolved Parliament in 1629, and for the next eleven years ruled without Parliament (the so-called 'Eleven Years' Tyranny') ... but money was a constant problem, and to make ends meet Charles was reduced to dredging up old taxes and taking forced loans.

In 1636 the king tried to collect an old tax called Ship Money. An MP named John Hampden refused to pay ... and everyone else followed suit.

Charles' Archbishop of Canterbury, William Laud, was also meeting resistance – the Puritans (see page 62) were furious with his attempts to reform the Church of England, saying they were just an attempt to bring back Catholicism. And when Laud tried to introduce his reforms into Scotland, the Scots rebelled.

Black Tom Tyrant

At this point, Charles called on Thomas Wentworth – the man who for the past eight years had been his ruthless Lord Deputy of Ireland, gaining the nickname 'Black Tom Tyrant'. Many MPs feared that Charles wanted him to establish in England a rule as ruthless as he had in Ireland.

Charles made Wentworth Earl of Strafford. However, as relations between the king and his MPs deteriorated, Parliament accused Strafford of treason and demanded his death. Rather than confront Parliament, the king abandoned his minister and Strafford was executed in May 1641.

Lucy the revolutionary

The Hays had known Wentworth for many years, because they had land in Ireland, and he admitted in a letter as early as 1635 that he 'admired and honoured' Lucy. After James Hay's death, Lucy and Wentworth grew very close, exchanged portraits ... and were even rumoured to be lovers. In 1641 Lucy was 42, and a mature, serious woman. Up until this point, she had been a **Royalist**. After Strafford's execution – according to one royalist writer – she became 'a she-saint', and started mixing with the **Parliamentarians**.

Meanwhile, the rift between king and Parliament was growing. In November 1641 MPs presented a Grand Remonstrance (a 'great protest') against Charles' rule. In a last-gasp attempt to stay in control, Charles went to Parliament on 4 January 1642, by surprise, with a troop of soldiers, to arrest the leading MP John Pym and four of his followers. But they were not there – 'the birds had flown', as Charles put it. They had been warned of his plans ... by Lucy Hay. Charles left London; in August he declared war on Parliament.

← A woodcut from the time showing the execution of the Earl of Strafford for treason.

C

← This painting was made by the Flemish painter Anthony Van Dyck, dated 1637. It shows Lucy Hay at the height of her fame and celebrity – if you want to know what the people of the 1630s considered 'sexy' – this is it. She sent this painting to Thomas Wentworth.

Think

Study painting C carefully.

▌ List the elements that make it a seductive portrayal of Lucy Hay.

▌ Why do you think she sent this painting to Wentworth?

Activity

1 Discuss in a group, share as a class, and record in your table what pages 68–69 tell us about:

Lucy Hay	Seventeenth-century women	Politics – the causes of the Civil War

2 Add the more important events you have learned about to your 'Timeline of events in the life of Lucy Hay'.

3 At this period of her life, was Lucy Hay merely reacting to events as they happened, or was she affecting events and 'making history' herself? Did *Lucy Hay* cause the Civil War?

5

What can Lucy Hay tell us about life during the English Civil War?

Lucy at war, 1642–48

War – or, to be more precise, the need to win a war – churns up society. It gives opportunities to new ideas and new people. These pages look at how Lucy Hay fared during the Civil War – would she sink, swim or prosper?

Choosing sides

A civil war is a messy thing. Many people found it difficult to decide who to fight for. In part it was a war between the **aristocracy** (for the king) and the 'middle class' (for Parliament) – see pages 8–9. It was also a war of the regions, with London and the south-east for Parliament, and the North, Wales and the West Country for the king. But, area-by-area, family-by-family, people made up their own minds. Son fought father; local rivals joined opposing sides. Some families put people on both sides so that – whatever happened – they would be on the winning side.

In 1642, the king advanced on London, but was turned back at Turnham Green when the citizens turned out to block the way. In 1643, a three-pronged Royalist attack on London was defeated.

Slowly, Parliament began to win. At the start of the war, many of the parliamentary commanders were hesitant; they did not want to get rid of the king altogether – they still wanted a monarchy. Oliver Cromwell, a general in Parliament's army, was outraged by this. He trained a 'New Model Army', and set about winning the war by whatever means necessary – at Marston Moor (1644), for example, he attacked the Royalists while they were having their tea! In 1645 he

persuaded Parliament to pass a Self-Denying Ordinance to sack the faint-heart generals, and he destroyed the Royalist army at Naseby. Charles was captured and imprisoned.

Lucy Hay, negotiator

Where was Lucy Hay in all this? Throughout the Civil War she was still a member of the royal court. But, as we saw, in 1641 she had decided to support Parliament. She and her close friend Lord Holland were useful to parliamentary leaders such as John Pym and Denzil Holles because they were able to reveal what the king and queen were saying and planning. She was accused of having affairs with both of them.

As the war went on, however, Lucy found herself more on the side of the parliamentary moderates, who wanted to negotiate with Charles, than the army extremists, who wanted to destroy him. Her connections with the court made her the perfect go-between. She stayed in contact with Henrietta Maria, who had fled to France in 1644, and hosted meetings between the French Ambassador, the king's supporters, and the parliamentary leaders.

D

Lucy Hay: diplomat or conspirator?

The Countess of Carlisle has sent to me to say that the Chancellor of Scotland had visited her, and had solemnly declared to her that he did not want to ruin the king, nor royalty. She assures me that she had seen into his real intentions, and she had dined with four lords from the Parliament, who on this subject had stated their desire for peace, and the re-establishment of the person and government of the king.

A report by the French Ambassador Sabran, 1644. Sabran was a close friend and adviser of Charles I's wife, Queen Henrietta Maria.

The Second Civil War

The king was defeated in 1645, but he and the moderate and more extreme Parliamentarians spent the next two years failing to agree a settlement. In December 1647, Charles made a treaty with the Scots, and launched a Second Civil War. This time, Lucy Hay supported him.

Lucy acted as co-ordinator for the scattered Royalist uprisings. She sold a pearl necklace for £1500 to pay for a troop of soldiers under Lord Holland to attack London. And – when the king's son, Charles Prince of Wales, sailed up the River Thames with nine ships – his contact in London was none other than … Lucy Hay.

E

← This painting of Lucy Hay was painted by the Flemish painter Anthony Van Dyck sometime between 1637 and 1640.

Think

The painting differs from Van Dyck's painting of Lucy on page 69. It portrays a slightly older Lucy Hay, and is trying to show a different side to her.

What kind of person do you think Van Dyck is trying to portray Lucy to be?

Activity

1 Study report D on page 70. What does it tell us about Lucy's role in the Civil War?

2 Discuss in a group, share as a class, and record on your table what pages 70–71 tell us about:

Lucy Hay	Seventeenth-century women	Politics – the events of the Civil War

3 Add the more important events you have learned about to your 'Timeline of events in the life of Lucy Hay'.

4 At this period of her life, was Lucy Hay merely reacting to events as they happened, or was she affecting events and 'making history' herself?

5

What can Lucy Hay tell us about life during the English Civil War?

Lucy soldiers on, 1649–60

Now it is time to review your learning for the whole section, and to move towards a final evaluation of Lucy, and of her influence.

Lucy in danger

The Second Civil War was a disaster for Charles. His Scottish army was defeated at the Battle of Preston, and the royalist uprisings fizzled out. Worse, Cromwell and the Parliamentarians' army were now determined to bring 'Charles Stuart, that man of blood, to account'. On 30 January 1649, Charles was executed (see pages 2–3) and England entered into the period of the **Interregnum**. After four years of rule by Parliament, in 1653 Oliver Cromwell seized power and established a military dictatorship.

In March 1649, Lucy was taken to the Tower, where she had lived as a child. She was shown the instruments of torture. But she was not tortured or executed. She spent eighteen months in the Tower, and another eighteen months after that under **house arrest**.

Lucy's last days

Remarkably, Lucy did not disappear from the political scene, even during the rule of Cromwell. And in 1660, she was one of those involved in the negotiations to bring back the monarchy – although she drove Charles II's agent to distraction, 'telling many lies of him every day' and immediately passing on to her friends everything she heard.

Nevertheless, when she died on 5 November 1660, she had lived to see the success of her final project, and Charles II restored to the throne.

F

The lady, at whose house you met, used to pride herself on her great beauty and her great talents; the years must have carried off the former, but I doubt if they have provided her with the latter.

Count de Brienne, French Secretary of State, writing to the Ambassador Sabran in 1644/45.

G

I am a litle scandalized I confess that she uses that word faithfull [at the end of her letters], she that never knew how to bee soe in her life.

Lady Dorothy Osborne, British writer (1653).

H

What might not the Countess of Carlisle have accomplished, had she not spoilt, by the weaknesses of the heart, all that she had obtained by her mind.

Charles St Évremond, French writer (1670). Évremond was writing to his young charge Hortense Mancini, whom he feared was risking her future by having an affair.

◄ When Alexandre Dumas wrote *The Three Musketeers* in 1844, he based the character of the beautiful, seductive, lying and ruthless 'Milady de Winter' on Lucy, Countess of Carlisle. (The picture shows actress Milla Jovovich, who played Milady in the 2011 Hollywood blockbuster.)

Women of the Civil War

Lucy Hay was not the only remarkable heroine of the Civil War.

> Lady Lucy Hutchinson nursed wounded soldiers of both sides.

> Jane Whorwood smuggled money and messages to Charles I in prison; at his execution, only she dared to cheer him.

> Anne Halkett risked her life helping Charles I's son, James, Duke of York, to escape to the continent.

> Mary Lady Bankes (Corfe Castle in Dorset), Charlotte Countess of Derby (Lathom House in Derbyshire), and Brilliana Harley (Brampton Bryan in Herefordshire) fought to defend their homes against the enemy.

> Margaret Fell was one of the founders of the **Quaker** movement.

⬆ This engraving of Lucy Hay was made by Flemish engraver Pieter de Bailliu sometime between 1646 and 1650 – when she was at the height of her influence.

Activity

1 Working in a small group, study in turn extracts F, G and H on page 72 and discuss the following.
   - How have the writers interpreted Lucy's character and influence?
   - Looking at who wrote each source, can you suggest why they wrote as they did?
   - Do you agree with what they said – were they correct?

2 Discuss in a group, share as a class, and record on your table what pages 72–73 tell us about:

Lucy Hay	Seventeenth-century women	Politics – 1649–1660

3 Add the more important events you have learned about to your 'Timeline of events in the life of Lucy Hay'.

4 At this period of her life, was Lucy Hay merely reacting to events as they happened, or was she affecting events and 'making history' herself?

5 Looking back over your 'Timeline of events in the life of Lucy Hay', choose the TEN most important events in Lucy's life, and turn them into a 'living graph' of ups and downs.

Lucy's eventful life

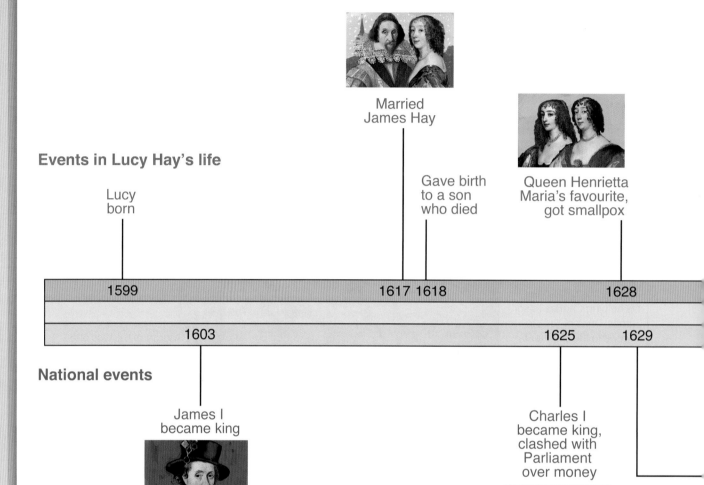

Events in Lucy Hay's life

Lucy born	Married James Hay	Queen Henrietta Maria's favourite, got smallpox
	Gave birth to a son who died	

| 1599 | 1617 1618 | 1628 |

| 1603 | 1625 | 1629 |

National events

James I became king

Charles I became king, clashed with Parliament over money

Activity

1 Review in your group, then share as a class, what you have learned in this section about:

 ▮ Lucy Hay: what is your interpretation of her character and influence (support your ideas with facts)?

 ▮ Seventeenth-century women.

 ▮ Seventeenth-century politics – politics at the court of Charles I, and the causes and events. Use the timeline on these pages to help you.

2 Study the timeline to get an overview of Lucy's life, then discuss as a whole class:

 ▮ Was Lucy ever the master of her own destiny, or did she just react to events?

 ▮ Were there any occasions when she 'made history'?

3 Poets praised and criticised Lucy Hay all her life (see page 66). Write your own: 'A poetic interpretation of Lucy Hay, Countess of Carlisle'.

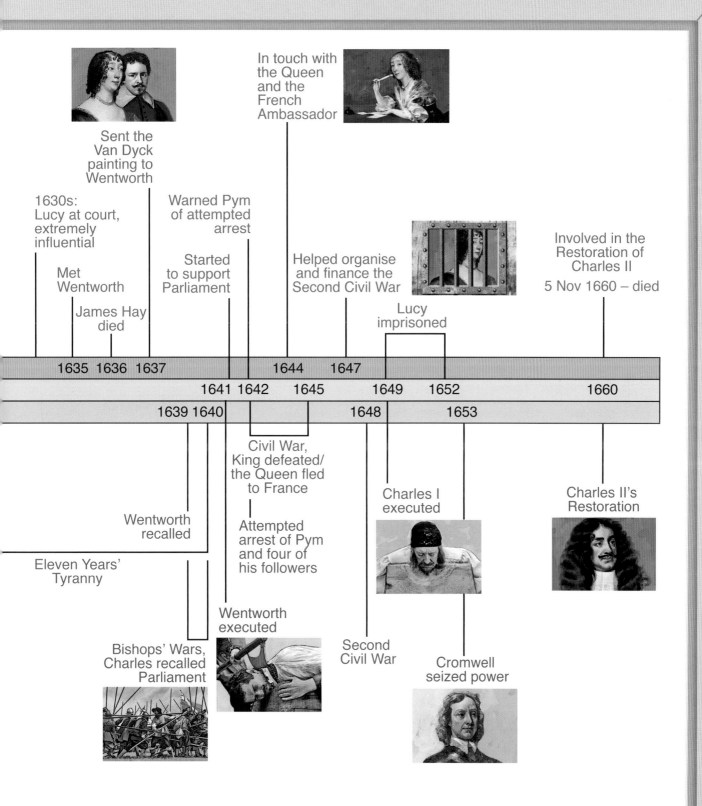

Sent the Van Dyck painting to Wentworth

In touch with the Queen and the French Ambassador

1630s: Lucy at court, extremely influential

Warned Pym of attempted arrest

Met Wentworth

Started to support Parliament

James Hay died

Helped organise and finance the Second Civil War

Lucy imprisoned

Involved in the Restoration of Charles II
5 Nov 1660 – died

1635 1636 1637   1644   1647

1641 1642   1645   1649   1652   1660

1639 1640   1648   1653

Civil War, King defeated/ the Queen fled to France

Wentworth recalled

Attempted arrest of Pym and four of his followers

Eleven Years' Tyranny

Charles I executed

Charles II's Restoration

Wentworth executed

Bishops' Wars, Charles recalled Parliament

Second Civil War

Cromwell seized power

6

Was the execution of Charles I significant in the history of royal power in England?

Was the execution of Charles I significant in the history of royal power in England?

What makes an event 'significant'?

So – what did you come up with in your discussion? What makes an event or person significant? It is more than just 'importance'. (History is full of people who were rich, famous, and of high rank ... who many would consider to be utterly insignificant!)

'Significance' is ultimately a judgement – an opinion. Different historians will have different views, and historians' interpretations of the significance of an event will change over time. That judgement will probably be based on the criteria in the picture below.

3 Permanence

Lasting effects: the most 'significant' historical events will be ones that still affect our lives today.

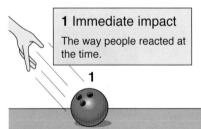

1 Immediate impact

The way people reacted at the time.

2 Effects

How the person or event changed things.

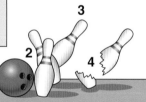

4 Importance

The *amount* of change: the bigger and wider the effect, the greater the significance.

Was 1649 a significant event? First thoughts

Now, in this section, you are going to decide whether the Civil War and the execution of Charles I was significant in the history of royal power in England.

Charles' death certainly created a reaction at the time! But does that make it 'significant'? What were the effects of the execution? How much did things change? And how long did the changes last – does the execution of Charles I still have an impact on who has power in the country today?

⬆ An engraving of Charles I's execution.

Activity

Rehearsing what you already know
1 Make a Notes Sheet by dividing a sheet of A3 paper into four quarters to create four cells. Give each cell a heading as shown in the example below.

1 Evidence of the immediate impact at the time	2 Effects – evidence that it changed things
3 Permanence – evidence about how long lasting the effects were	4 Importance – evidence about how much it changed things

Working with a partner or in a small group, look back through pages 2–3 and 72, and collect evidence of the impact of the king's execution at the time. Share your results as a whole class and note the best ideas onto your Notes Sheet in cell **1: Evidence of the immediate impact at the time**. (You will be returning to extend your notes on this throughout the section.)

2 Here is a list of the topics we will be studying in the rest of this section. Working as a whole class, discuss how each topic might help you to form a judgement about the significance of the king's execution in 1649 – about the impact it had at the time, the effects it had, and how big and lasting those effects were:
   a) Resistance to royal power, 1509–1745.
   b) The growing power of Parliament, 1509–1745, and its conflicts with the monarch.
   c) England's government immediately after the execution, 1649–60.
   d) Radical and revolutionary groups which sprang up during the Civil War period.
   e) The Glorious Revolution of 1688 and changes in government, 1688–1745.

6

Was the execution of Charles I significant in the history of royal power in England?

Was 1649 a significant challenge to royal power?

If we are going to study the significance of the Civil War and the execution of the king, the first thing we need to do is to compare it to other uprisings of the time.

Activity

The table opposite lists fifteen revolutions, rebellions and plots in the years 1509–1745.

Working as an individual or in a small group:

1 Make a timeline showing the years 1509–1745. Mark onto the timeline a dot in the correct place for each of the fifteen rebellions.

2 Using the information in the table to give you ideas, make a list of factors which made a rebellion 'dangerous' for the monarch. Then discuss each rebellion in turn. Give each rebellion a 'dangerousness' mark out of ten and draw it onto the timeline as a bar graph.

3 The Civil War (1642–49) was clearly very different to all the other rebellions and plots; make a list of FOUR differences.

4 Coming together as a whole class, discuss whether 1649 changed anything. Can you find any ways in which the rebellions after 1649 were different – for example, more dangerous or frequent, had different aims, people and so on – from those before 1649?

5 Go back to the Notes Sheet that you started on page 77. Note your best ideas onto the sheet in cell **2: Effects – evidence that it changed things**.

Was 1649 significant?

When the authors of this book drew the 'dangerousness' bar graph exercise in Excel it looked something like this:

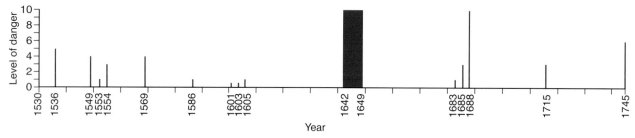

We think it shows beyond doubt that the Civil War was longer, bigger and (apart from the Glorious Revolution) more successful than any other rebellion in the period. But did it change anything? It seemed to us that the rebellions after 1649 were no different to those before 1649, either in frequency or dangerousness.

Certainly, we felt that royal power was no more or no less vulnerable to plots and rebellions after 1649 than it had been before 1649. So, if the Civil War changed nothing, then should we conclude that it was not significant? Maybe it is too early for you to decide? Let's continue our investigation and see whether we think 1649 was a significant event in the history of Parliament.

Year	Resistance	Cause	Extent	Result
1536	**Pilgrimage of Grace**	A demonstration against the dissolution of the monasteries	30,000 protestors across the North of England, especially Yorkshire and Lincolnshire	The rebels captured York, but disbanded when the king promised an amnesty
1549	**Prayer Book Rebellion**	A rebellion against Edward VI's religious changes	7000 armed rebels in Cornwall and Devon	The royal army massacred the rebels
1553	**Lady Jane Grey plot**	An attempt to stop Mary becoming queen	The Earl of Northumberland had an army of 1500 retainers	The attempt collapsed; Northumberland and Lady Jane were executed
1554	**Wyatt's Rebellion**	A rebellion against Queen Mary's 'Spanish marriage' to Philip II	4000 rebels across four counties, including a number of nobles	Only the rebellion in Kent took place; it surrendered after the first battle
1569	**Northern Earls' Rebellion**	An attempt by Catholic nobles to depose Elizabeth I	About 4500 rebels across Northumberland, Durham and Cumberland	The rebels captured Durham, but were stopped by a larger royal army and fled
1586	**Babington Plot**	The last of four plots to kill Elizabeth I and crown Mary Queen of Scots	Small numbers of conspirators	Easily uncovered by Elizabeth's agents. The leaders were executed
1601	**Essex's Rebellion**	Lord Essex was disgruntled by his treatment by Queen Elizabeth I	He and armed friends rode to London demanding to see the queen	Essex was arrested and beheaded
1603	**Main and Bye Plots**	Plots to dethrone James I	Small numbers of conspirators	Easily uncovered, and the ringleaders were executed
1605	**Gunpowder Plot**	Plot to blow up Parliament	Thirteen conspirators	The plotters were discovered and executed as an example
1642–49	**Civil War**	Parliament fought against the king	Nationwide	Ended with the execution of Charles I
1683	**Rye House Plot**	Plot to assassinate Charles II	40 main plotters with links to many other rebel groups	Betrayed; the plotters were imprisoned or executed
1685	**Monmouth Rebellion**	Plot to dethrone James II	4000 rebels, mostly from Somerset	Defeated at the Battle of Sedgemoor; 300 rebels hanged
1688	**Glorious Revolution**	Seven lords invited William of Orange to invade and depose James II	William had a fleet of 463 ships and an army of 40,000	William successfully deposed James II
1715	**The Fifteen Rebellion**	Plot to depose King George I and restore the Stuarts	An army of 5000 Scots rebelled; in England, only small numbers joined	The Scots were defeated at the Battle of Sheriffmuir; the English rebels were routed at the Battle of Preston
1745	**The Forty-Five Rebellion**	Plot to depose King George II and restore the Stuarts	An army of 5000 Scots invaded England; no Englishmen joined them	The Scots reached Derby, but turned back and were defeated at Culloden in 1746

6

Was the execution of Charles I significant in the history of royal power in England?

Where does 1649 fit into Parliament's history?

Although Parliament's influence had been gradually growing throughout the Middle Ages, it was not nearly so important as later in history – the king just closed Parliament down if the MPs caused trouble and ordinary people had little say in government. You are now going to look at the development of Parliament, 1509–1745, and evaluate the significance of the execution of Charles in that process.

Certainly, when you compare the picture of Henry VIII's Parliament in 1525 (picture A below) to Pine's engraving of Parliament in 1741 (picture B opposite), you cannot help but be struck by how much the government had changed in those 200 years.

A

This picture shows Henry VIII in Parliament in 1525:

1 The king is seated on the throne.

2 To the king's right are his chancellor and the two archbishops.

3 On the king's left are two officers of the royal household (in black).

4 The **Garter King of Arms** (who was Thomas Wriothesley, for whom the painting was made).

5 The two leading noblemen of the realm in their red robes.

6 The bishops and abbots are seated on the left.

7 The nobles are seated on the right.

The four woolsacks in the middle are a symbol of the wool trade; the officers of the Parliament sit on the woolsacks:

8 Two chief justices.

9 The judges and Serjeants of the law.

10 Two clerks with their quills and inkpots.

11 At the bar of the House stands the Speaker of the House of Commons.

B

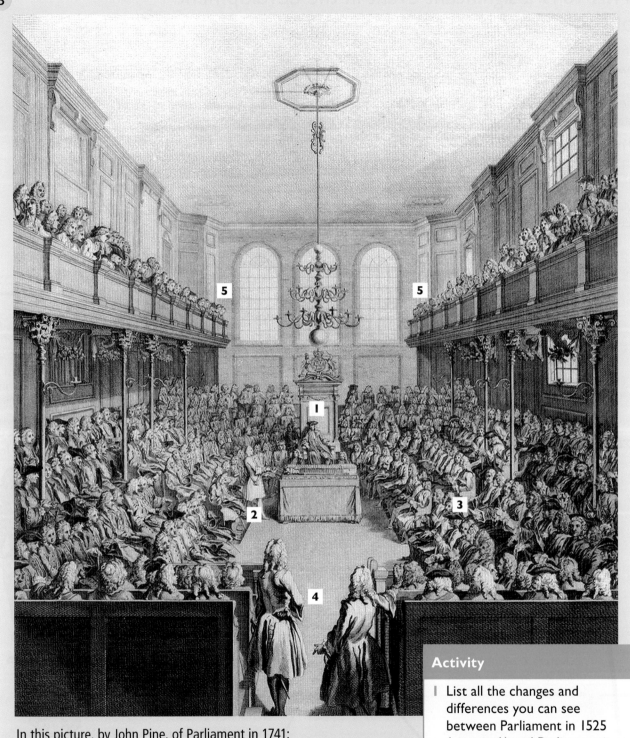

In this picture, by John Pine, of Parliament in 1741:

1 The session is controlled by Arthur Onslow, the Speaker.

2 The government is represented by the Prime Minister Robert Walpole.

3 He is opposed, formally, by **His Majesty's Opposition**.

4 The debates are free and are decided by a vote – the two people standing in the foreground may be the 'tellers' who counted the votes.

5 From galleries, the public watch their government in action.

Activity

1 List all the changes and differences you can see between Parliament in 1525 (picture A) and Parliament in 1741 (picture B).

2 What does picture A on page 80 suggest about Parliament in the sixteenth century?

3 What does picture B suggest about Parliament in the eighteenth century?

6

Was the execution of Charles I significant in the history of royal power in England?

Was 1649 a significant event in the development of Parliament?

If we are going to study the significance of the Civil War and the execution of the king, the second thing we need to do is to see those events in the wider context of the development of Parliament, and to decide for yourself whether – and how much – each event stands out as a 'significant' event in that process.

This timeline shows fifteen occasions when Parliament clashed with the monarch, between 1509 and 1745. These events could be regarded as 'milestones' on the road to Parliamentary government.

Studying the timeline will allow you to form an opinion about whether the Civil War and the execution of the king changed anything.

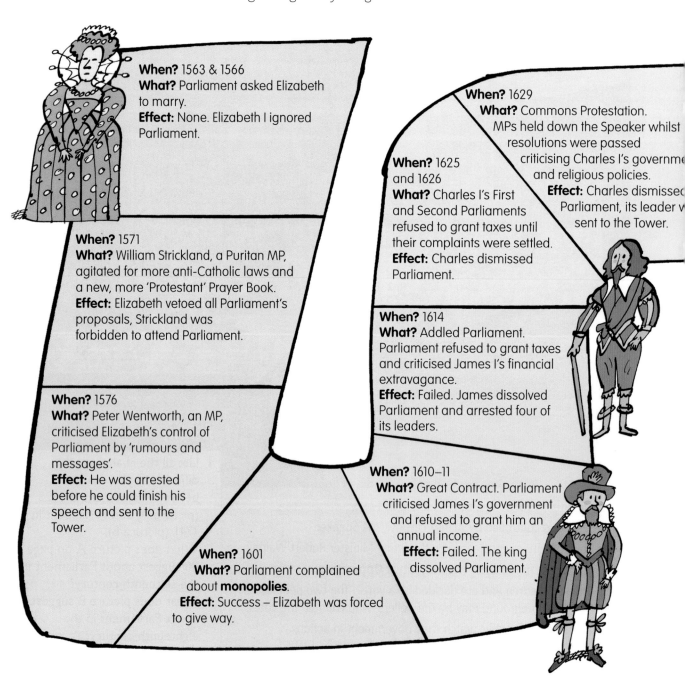

When? 1563 & 1566
What? Parliament asked Elizabeth to marry.
Effect: None. Elizabeth I ignored Parliament.

When? 1571
What? William Strickland, a Puritan MP, agitated for more anti-Catholic laws and a new, more 'Protestant' Prayer Book.
Effect: Elizabeth vetoed all Parliament's proposals, Strickland was forbidden to attend Parliament.

When? 1576
What? Peter Wentworth, an MP, criticised Elizabeth's control of Parliament by 'rumours and messages'.
Effect: He was arrested before he could finish his speech and sent to the Tower.

When? 1601
What? Parliament complained about **monopolies**.
Effect: Success – Elizabeth was forced to give way.

When? 1610–11
What? Great Contract. Parliament criticised James I's government and refused to grant him an annual income.
Effect: Failed. The king dissolved Parliament.

When? 1614
What? Addled Parliament. Parliament refused to grant taxes and criticised James I's financial extravagance.
Effect: Failed. James dissolved Parliament and arrested four of its leaders.

When? 1625 and 1626
What? Charles I's First and Second Parliaments refused to grant taxes until their complaints were settled.
Effect: Charles dismissed Parliament.

When? 1629
What? Commons Protestation. MPs held down the Speaker whilst resolutions were passed criticising Charles I's governme[nt] and religious policies.
Effect: Charles dismissed Parliament, its leader w[as] sent to the Tower.

Activity

Working in a small group, study the fifteen occasions on pages 82–83 when Parliament clashed with the monarch, then:

1 Divide them into 'Parliament's successes' and 'Parliament's failures'.
2 Make a list of the issues over which monarch and Parliament quarrelled – in particular, note the occasions when money matters soured relations between monarch and Parliament.
3 Working as a whole class, discuss what would you regard as the most significant milestone in the development of Parliament's power in this period. Justify your choice.
4 Does the timeline seem to show a gradual growth in Parliament's power or a sudden, unexpected breakdown of relations in 1649?
5 Does the evidence support the idea that 1649 was 'a turning point' in the monarch's power?

When? 1642–49
What? Civil War. Parliament fought against the king.
Effect: War ended with the execution of Charles I.

When? 1649–60
What? Protectorate Parliaments.
Effect: Cromwell called four Parliaments – and dismissed them because they were too troublesome.

When? 1673
What? Test Act. Parliament forced Charles II to introduce a Test Act forbidding Catholics to hold office.
Effect: Successful: Charles had to agree and James Duke of York was forced to resign as Lord High Admiral.

When? 1679
What? Habeas Corpus. Parliament passed a law that no citizen could be imprisoned without being charged with a crime.
Effect: Passed to stop Charles II arresting his opponents, it survived until the Terrorism Act of 2005.

When? 1679–81
What? Exclusion Crisis. A public campaign to try to prevent James II taking the throne when Charles II died.
Effect: Defeated when Charles dissolved Parliament and sent the leader Lord Shaftesbury to the Tower.

When? 1689 and 1697
What? Bill of Rights and Civil List.
Effect: The Bill of Rights permanently limited the power of the monarch.
The civil list – a money grant to the king – made the monarch totally dependent on Parliament.

When? 1714
What? George I, who spoke little English, entrusted the government to a 'prime minister', Robert Walpole.
Effect: The beginning of Parliamentary government.

6

Was the execution of Charles I significant in the history of royal power in England?

The Whig interpretation of Parliament's power, 1509–1745

The Whig historians of the late nineteenth and early twentieth centuries (see page 11) would have had no difficulty at all answering our question: Was 1649 a significant event?

For them, the issue was what we today would call a 'no-brainer'! Living as they did in a Parliamentary democracy, they looked back on history, saw Parliament's power growing gradually through the centuries, and decided that the growth of Parliament was unstoppable and inevitable – even destined. They saw the Civil War and the death of Charles as inevitable – they believed the Stuarts got their comeuppance because they foolishly tried to stand against the unstoppable growth of Parliament. You can see their views on the Tudors and Stuarts below.

The Tudors

> Henry VIII, Edward VI and Mary all used Parliament to introduce their religious changes, so Parliament grew in importance under the Tudors. When Queen Elizabeth came in, she brilliantly and wisely controlled her Parliaments by co-operation not force.

The early Stuarts

> The Stuarts were bad kings. Coming from Scotland, they did not understand England's parliamentary system. Instead, they believed in **Divine Right** – that they were appointed by God to be 'absolute rulers'.

> As a result, James I and Charles I increasingly fell out with their Parliaments, until eventually Charles I dismissed Parliament altogether and ruled alone during his Eleven Years' Tyranny.

> So Parliament was forced to go to Civil War with the king, and – after he treacherously caused the Second Civil War – to chop off his head in 1649. This was a key moment in the history of Parliament – the time when England said 'No' to **absolutism**.

The later Stuarts

> After 1649, England fell under an army dictatorship (see pages 86–87), and people were glad to bring back Charles II in 1660.

> The Stuarts were incorrigible, and set about again trying to bring back Catholicism and absolutism. But the British people were not prepared to return to tyranny. They drove out James II in the 'Glorious Revolution' of 1688 (see pages 90–91), and established a Protestant succession and a 'constitutional monarchy' – which together formed the basis of Great Britain's future greatness.

Challenging the Whigs

For the Whig historians, the Civil War was the moment when British people stood up and said 'No' to tyranny. The soldiers of the Parliamentary armies were the heroes who bought our freedom with their blood, and 1649 was a turning point in the history of the nation.

But were the Whig historians right?

Recent revisionist historians have interpreted the Civil War differently … as a sudden and even unnecessary conflict caused by an incompetent king. If Charles had not tried to arrest the five members in 1642, Parliament would not have responded with the Nineteen Propositions, and there would not have been a Civil War at all. Apart from Charles I, their argument goes, relations between king and Parliament were fractious, but manageable.

For the revisionists, the Civil War was a mistake of history, corrected by 1660 and the Restoration of Charles II … and the events which established Parliamentary government came later – in 1688, 1689 and 1714.

So whether we believe the Whigs or the revisionists will affect our judgement about the significance of 1649, and whether it was a turning point in history, or an historical wrong turn.

Activity

In a small group, discuss the following, supporting your opinions with facts and arguments:

1 Looking at the evidence on pages 82–83, would you say that the growth of Parliament was:
  - gradual
  - unstoppable
  - inevitable?

2 Did Elizabeth 'brilliantly and wisely control her Parliaments by co-operation not force'?

3 Looking at the evidence on pages 64–65 and 82–83, would you agree with the Whigs that:
  - the Stuart kings were to blame for the Civil Wars
  - the Civil War was the result of a gradual growth in Parliament's power, not of a sudden, unexpected breakdown of relations in 1642?

4 Coming together as a whole class, discuss:
  - From what you have learned so far, whom do you agree with – Whigs or revisionists?
  - Was 1649 a turning point, or a wrong turn, in British history?

5 Access the Notes Sheet that you started on page 77. Note your best ideas onto the sheet in cell **4: Importance – evidence about how much it changed things**.

Was the execution of Charles I significant in the history of royal power in England?

6

What were the immediate effects of 1649?

You saw on pages 76–77 that, if you are to decide whether Charles I's execution was a significant event in history, you will need to look at its effects. Pages 86–89 therefore look at the immediate results of the death of the king, and ask you to evaluate how significant they were.

The Interregnum

The eleven years after Charles was executed are called the **Interregnum**. The period was anything BUT a step forward for Parliament! Rather, it was a victory for the army, and for the years 1649–60 England was ruled by an army dictatorship led by the Parliamentary general Oliver Cromwell.

In 1649 Cromwell crushed the Irish in a brutal war which included the massacres of the inhabitants of the towns of Drogheda and Wexford – the Irish were Catholics, and were treated without mercy. The Irish campaign was followed in 1650 by a successful campaign to defeat the Scots.

By this time, the Parliament meeting in London was the same group of MPs who had been called by Charles I in 1640 – by 1653 there were only 50 of them left. So Cromwell took a troop of soldiers and sent Parliament away.

Cromwell wanted England to be a godly state, ruled according to Protestant principles (see page 41). Therefore, in July 1653 he called 140 godly men from all over the country, and set them up as a 'Parliament of saints'. It is often called the 'Barebones' Parliament after the name of the first MP on the list, who was called Praisegod Barebones. But the Parliament was a disaster – the saints spent all their time arguing, and after five months Cromwell sent them home.

Cromwell dismissed his next Parliament (1654) when it refused to agree to his position as **Lord Protector**. Instead he tried ruling through a system of military governors. The Major-Generals imposed strict Puritan morals, banned pastimes such as football and horse-racing, closed ale-houses and theatres, and even passed a law forbidding people to celebrate Christmas day. The Major-Generals were hated, however, and had to be phased out.

C

An Allegory of events surrounding King Charles I in 1649 shows what many people felt at the time.

- The ship represents the government (the 'ship of state'). What is happening to it?
- What are the sailors doing to their captain?
- How are 'the people' reacting?
- Who, ominously, waits behind the people on the right, ready to take over?
- What is happening to the Church?
- What does God think about it all?
- How many symbols of doom can you spot?

Cromwell's successes

Cromwell called another Parliament in 1656. It asked him to declare himself king, but he refused. In the end Cromwell failed to find a system of government which worked.

In other ways, however, Cromwell's regime was quite successful. He allowed Jews to return to England (for the first time since 1290). He also reduced the number of crimes which carried the death penalty.

It was in his foreign policy that he was probably most successful. He defeated the Dutch in a short war in 1654, established English control of the seas around England, and forbade the Dutch to trade with English colonies. Then he made an alliance with France and went to war against Spain … and in May 1655 the navy captured the Spanish island of Jamaica in the West Indies.

Historians have suggested that, in this way, Cromwell began the building of the British Empire, Britain's domination of world trade, and of a British navy which 'ruled the waves'.

Even so, many people hated Cromwell as a tyrant and, after his death, they were happy to restore Charles II to the throne.

Activity

Working as a whole class;
1 Pictures C and D on pages 86–87 are both 'allegories' – there is a meaning in the things that are happening in the picture. Explain the allegories.
2 Discuss the results of the execution of the king between 1649 and 1660. Note your best ideas onto the Notes Sheet you started on page 77 in cell **2: Effects – evidence that it changed things**.
3 Discuss the following.
   ▌ How long did the immediate effects of the execution of the king last?
   ▌ Did 1649 mark the end of royal power?
   ▌ Was 1649 a step forward for British democracy?
   Note your best ideas onto your Notes Sheet in cell **3: Permanence – evidence about how long lasting the effects were**.

D

← In this allegorical Dutch woodcut from the late 1650s, entitled *King Oliver*, Cromwell is being crowned by a griffin (a symbol of Satan) – not just with a royal crown, but with the papal crown. He is crushing a Scotsman under his foot, and an Irishman between his knees, whilst he disembowels a Dutchman and holds a Frenchman under his arm. On the wall, there are pictures showing the execution of Charles I, and Cromwell meeting people, burning Dutch ships and the English lion defeating its enemies.

6

Was the execution of Charles I significant in the history of royal power in England?

The world turned upside down?

Whilst Oliver Cromwell was experimenting with new kinds of government, the death of the King had also unleashed an explosion of **radical** political and religious ideas (see page 89). It was as though the removal of the traditional authority of a monarch freed people – albeit only for a short time – to explore alternative beliefs and lifestyles … and led to some very radical groups.

If we are assessing the effects of 1649 as part of our study of the significance of the execution of the king, then we need to assess the significance of these radical groups and their ideas.

Radicalism defeated

In the end, most of the radical groups were forcibly suppressed. When the cult leader James Nayler rode into Bristol on a donkey in 1656 (like Christ rode into Jerusalem on Palm Sunday), Parliament wanted to execute him; in the end they settled for putting him in the **pillory**, whipping him through the streets of London and Bristol, branding him with the letter B (for 'blasphemer'), piercing his tongue with a hot iron, and sentencing him to two years' hard labour.

Faced by persecution, the radical groups disappeared; their supporters melted away. Only the Quakers survived, and they did so by becoming respectable and keeping out of politics.

> **Think**
>
> It seemed to the author of the 1646 pamphlet below that the world had 'turned upside down'. Can you spot:
> - EIGHT examples of things which are 'the wrong way round'?
> - THREE instances where there has been a change in authority, and the weak have 'turned the tables' on the strong?

E

THE

World turn'd upfide down:

OR,

A briefe defcription of the ridiculous Fafhions of thefe diftracted Times.

By T.J. a well-willer to King, Parliament and Kingdom.

London : Printed for *John Smith*. 1647.

Christopher Hill

Christopher Hill was one of the **Marxist** historians of the twentieth century (see page 11). Hill specialised in the Civil War period, but he largely ignored the struggle between king and Parliament. He saw the Civil War instead as a time of 'teeming freedom', when ordinary people found their voice, and the country bristled with radical, revolutionary ideas. He called this explosion of ideas 'the revolt within the revolution'. Hill believed that it was these people who laid the foundations of our freedom and democracy. He accepted that the radical groups disappeared without trace after a very short while, but he thought that, although the groups were suppressed, their ideas lived on and surfaced again in the late eighteenth century, and set Britain on the path to real democracy.

Some of the radical groups of the Civil War

Levellers
Programme: Wanted annual elections, the vote for all men, education for all, equality, and freedom of speech and worship.
Leader: John Lilburne, but many were women.
Effect: Cromwell suppressed them in 1649, executing some, imprisoning others, and their support evaporated.

Diggers
Programme: The first **communists** – they wanted to share equally the work and the produce of the land. In 1649–50 they founded a number of communes.
Leader: Gerard Winstanley
Effect: Local landowners hired thugs to beat them up and drive them off the land.

Fifth Monarchists
Programme: Believed the reign of Christ had to be brought in by violence. In 1661 Thomas Venner led a small rebellion.
Leader: Led by Puritan preachers, including Thomas Venner.
Effect: Venner and ten others were hanged, drawn and quartered, and the sect disappeared.

Ranters
Programme: Believed that it was good to sin, and behaved immorally wherever possible.
Leader: No leader, no organisation.
Effect: Some historians believe they never existed, and were made up to frighten people.

Quakers
Programme: Anyone could speak at their meetings, during which they often became so filled with the Holy Spirit that they shook.
Leader: Their founder was George Fox, but many of their leaders were women.
Effect: There were about 30,000 Quakers in 1660. Quakerism was forbidden in 1662–89, but still survives as a religion today.

Activity

1 Study pages 88–89 then, working as a whole class, discuss the following question:

   Which of the radical groups' ideas still survive today?

   Add your best ideas onto your Notes Sheet you started on page 77 in cell **3: Permanence – evidence about how long lasting the effects were.**

2 Then discuss:
   ▌ Did the radical groups 'turn the world upside down'?
   ▌ Were the radical groups a step forward for British democracy?
   ▌ Which group was the MOST radical – the biggest threat to the establishment?

   Add your best ideas onto the Notes Sheet in cell **4: Importance – evidence about how much it changed things.**

6

Was the execution of Charles I significant in the history of royal power in England?

What happened in the Glorious Revolution of 1688?

6 On 10 June 1688, James' wife gave birth to a healthy boy. People were horrified. Some claimed the child had been smuggled into the bedroom in a warming pan.

7 On 30 June 1688, seven Protestant nobles invited William of Orange, Stadtholder of the Dutch Republic and husband of James II's daughter Mary, to invade.

8 On 5 November 1688, William landed at Torbay with a fleet of 463 ships and an army of 40,000 – an invasion twice the size of the Armada of 1588 (see pages 128–131).

Laws and liberties are openly transgressed and annulled; more especially an alteration of religion is endeavoured.

9 James's supporters deserted or joined William. William allowed James to escape to France, and he and Mary were given the crown jointly by Parliament.

Activity

Working with a partner or in a small group, read the story on pages 90–91 then discuss the following.
1 Why were English Protestants so horrified when James' son was born in June 1688?
2 What do you think were the causes of the 1688 revolution?
3 Why was James so easily defeated?
4 How 'glorious' was the Glorious Revolution?

6

Was the execution of Charles I significant in the history of royal power in England?

How did the government change after 1688?

In this chapter, you will consider what happened to the government of Britain after 1688 and finish your study on the significance of the execution of Charles I.

The Bill of Rights

Parliament had played almost no part in the removal of James II and almost didn't support the revolution at all. Having finally (6 February 1689) agreed that William and Mary were the rightful monarchs, however, Parliament then decided (as it said), 'to secure ourselves for the future'.

Consequently, in the (new) **coronation oath**, William and Mary promised, for the first time, to govern the people of England 'according to the laws in Parliament agreed on'. Then, in December 1689 Parliament passed a Bill of Rights. In it, William and Mary agreed:

- to call frequent Parliaments
- to allow MPs freedom of speech
- not to keep a standing army
- to let Parliament appoint the judges.

The civil list

Parliament took more control over the king in 1697 when it passed the civil list. This measure ended the constant trouble between monarch and Parliament over money matters. William was given an annual sum of £700,000 to run the government; but if he wanted any more (for instance, to go to war), he had to ask Parliament for the money. There is a saying: 'he who pays the piper calls the tune', and control of the purse-strings gave Parliament effective control over the king.

The Prime Minister

In 1714, royal power suffered another setback. Queen Anne did not have an immediate heir so – fearing that James II or his son might try to take back the throne – in 1701 Parliament passed the Act of Settlement. By its terms, when Anne died, the crown passed to George, ruler of the tiny German state of Hanover, *because he was a Protestant*. For George, becoming King of England was a huge step up, and – speaking little English – he soon started letting his first (or 'prime') minister, Robert Walpole, run the day-to-day government of the country. By the time George's grandson became king in 1760, it was too late – Parliament ruled, not the king.

F

⬆ This 1728 painting shows Arthur Onslow, the Speaker, asking Robert Walpole, the Prime Minister, to speak. Walpole has his hand casually in his pocket. What does this suggest about Parliament in the eighteenth century?

Activity

1 The three measures described on this page were immensely significant for royal power in England but had nothing to do with 1649. Working as a whole class, use this information to add negative comments onto the Notes Sheet you started on page 77 in cell **4: Importance – evidence about how much the execution of Charles I changed things**.

This section has studied the development of royal power from 1509 to 1745, trying to see the significance – if any – of 1649 within that process.

So now is the time to pull all your ideas together, and to come to a conclusion about the significance of the execution of Charles I as an historical event.

Activity

2 Split the class into groups.

▌ Some groups assemble all the facts and arguments they can find which suggest that Charles' execution was a 'game-changer' event in the history of the period, with big, important, long-lasting effects which changed history.

▌ Other groups work to prepare a convincing argument that Charles' execution was unimportant, limited and irrelevant to the way the country was governed.

Have a debate – how significant an event was 1649 in the history of royal power?

3 Write an essay to answer the question:

Was the execution of Charles I significant in the history of royal power in England?

▌ Start by writing a paragraph about the importance of the impact of the king's execution at the time, using the ideas you have gathered on your Notes Sheet in cell **1: Evidence of the immediate impact at the time**.

▌ Then write a paragraph about what was changed by the execution, using the ideas you have gathered on your Notes Sheet in cell **2: Effects – evidence that it changed things**.

▌ Next, write a paragraph about how long the effects of 1649 lasted, using the ideas you have gathered on your Notes Sheet in cell **3: Permanence – evidence about how long lasting the effects were**.

▌ Your next paragraph will be a discussion of how much the execution of Charles changed things. Use the ideas you have gathered on your Notes Sheet in cell **4: Importance – evidence about how much it changed things**. You will need to mention how the Whigs interpreted 1649, as well as the arguments that later developments were more important.

▌ Finally, write a conclusion. Were the authors right when we chose 1649 as the 'defining event' of the age? Was the execution of Charles I significant in the history of royal power in England? Explain your decision, taking into account what you have written about the immediate impact, effects, permanence and importance of the execution of Charles I.

King and Parliament through the ages

In the Middle Ages

Parliament not nearly as important as later.

The King just closed down Parliament if the MPs caused trouble.

Ordinary people had little say in government.

PARLIAMENT

In the reign of James I

Main, Bye and Gunpowder Plots.

PARLIAMENT

James I increasingly fell out with his Parliament.

Great contract.

Addled Parliament.

In the reign of George I

The Fifteen Rebellion.

A Protestant succession and a constitutional monarchy.

Public galleries.

The Speaker controlled the sessions.

PARLIAMENT

His Majesty's Opposition opposed the government.

The Prime Minister ran the government.

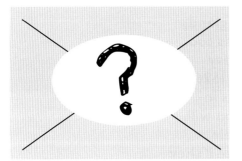

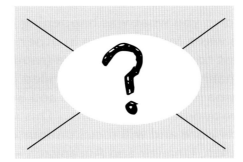

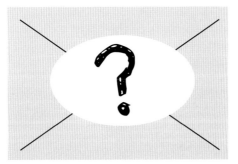

Activity

The illustrations on page 94 are simple visual representations of the relationship between monarch and Parliament in the Middle Ages, in the reign of James I, and in the reign of George I.

1 Working in a small group, using pages 65 and 82–83, choose THREE other monarchs whose reigns you judge to be significant moments in the story of Parliament.

2 For each of your chosen monarchs, decide what relationship they had with Parliament, then design and draw your own spider diagrams to illustrate that relationship, copying the style of the illustrations on page 94.

3 You now have a history of the relationship between king and Parliament in six spider diagrams! Present them as a display in chronological order (you will need to copy out the three on page 94 to do so), and take it in turns to explain the sequence as a narrative story, using phrases such as:

   It started with … but then … by this time … eventually … in the end…

4 Using the six key moments you have chosen, choreograph a dance for two dancers to show the developing relations between Parliament and the Crown.

   ▌ How will the dancers treat each other at the different points in the story?

   ▌ What kind of music might you use for the different sections of the dance?

7

Were the Mughals more successful than the Tudors and Stuarts?

Who was the greatest superpower of the sixteenth century?

This book so far has shown you what was happening in England, but in this period there was a lot happening in other places too. This section will look east to the Mughal Empire (modern day India, Pakistan and Afghanistan). The Mughals ruled from 1526 to 1857. They faced the same issues as the Tudors and Stuarts in England, but came up with different solutions. This section will look at who the Mughals were and will focus on four of their leaders – Akbar, Shah Jahan, Jahangir and Aurangzeb – to see if they were more or less successful than their English counterparts.

We will start by looking at the different global superpowers of the early sixteenth century as this will be a good introduction to get you thinking about whether they were more or less successful than the English.

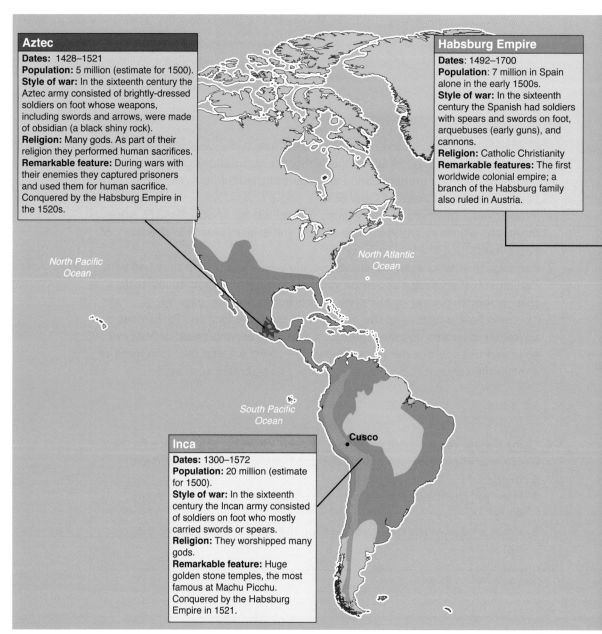

Aztec
Dates: 1428–1521
Population: 5 million (estimate for 1500).
Style of war: In the sixteenth century the Aztec army consisted of brightly-dressed soldiers on foot whose weapons, including swords and arrows, were made of obsidian (a black shiny rock).
Religion: Many gods. As part of their religion they performed human sacrifices.
Remarkable feature: During wars with their enemies they captured prisoners and used them for human sacrifice. Conquered by the Habsburg Empire in the 1520s.

Habsburg Empire
Dates: 1492–1700
Population: 7 million in Spain alone in the early 1500s.
Style of war: In the sixteenth century the Spanish had soldiers with spears and swords on foot, arquebuses (early guns), and cannons.
Religion: Catholic Christianity
Remarkable features: The first worldwide colonial empire; a branch of the Habsburg family also ruled in Austria.

North Pacific Ocean

North Atlantic Ocean

South Pacific Ocean

Cusco

Inca
Dates: 1300–1572
Population: 20 million (estimate for 1500).
Style of war: In the sixteenth century the Incan army consisted of soldiers on foot who mostly carried swords or spears.
Religion: They worshipped many gods.
Remarkable feature: Huge golden stone temples, the most famous at Machu Picchu. Conquered by the Habsburg Empire in 1521.

Activity

1 Based on the information on pages 96–97, make a list of the top five most powerful empires of the early sixteenth century. Where did England come on your list?
2 What criteria did you use? Would different criteria have produced a different order?
3 What other information would you need about these superpowers to make a more reasoned conclusion about which was the most powerful?

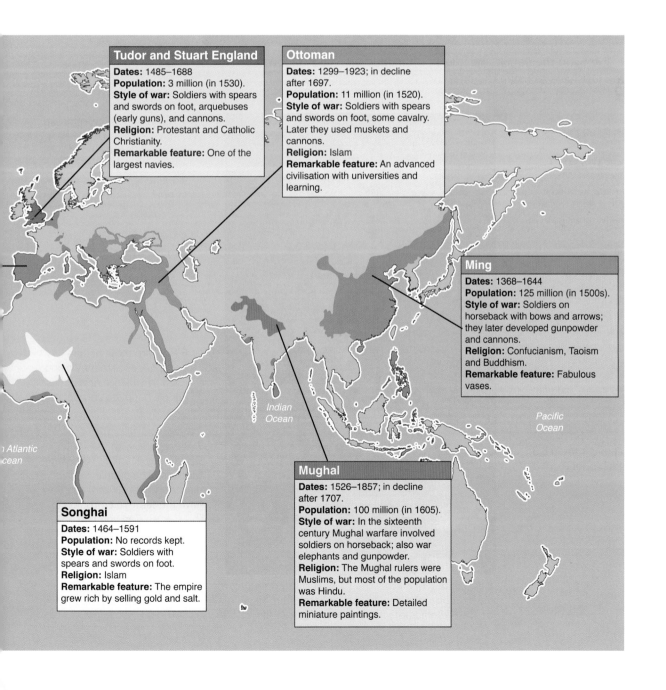

Tudor and Stuart England
Dates: 1485–1688
Population: 3 million (in 1530).
Style of war: Soldiers with spears and swords on foot, arquebuses (early guns), and cannons.
Religion: Protestant and Catholic Christianity.
Remarkable feature: One of the largest navies.

Ottoman
Dates: 1299–1923; in decline after 1697.
Population: 11 million (in 1520).
Style of war: Soldiers with spears and swords on foot, some cavalry. Later they used muskets and cannons.
Religion: Islam
Remarkable feature: An advanced civilisation with universities and learning.

Ming
Dates: 1368–1644
Population: 125 million (in 1500s).
Style of war: Soldiers on horseback with bows and arrows; they later developed gunpowder and cannons.
Religion: Confucianism, Taoism and Buddhism.
Remarkable feature: Fabulous vases.

Songhai
Dates: 1464–1591
Population: No records kept.
Style of war: Soldiers with spears and swords on foot.
Religion: Islam
Remarkable feature: The empire grew rich by selling gold and salt.

Mughal
Dates: 1526–1857; in decline after 1707.
Population: 100 million (in 1605).
Style of war: In the sixteenth century Mughal warfare involved soldiers on horseback; also war elephants and gunpowder.
Religion: The Mughal rulers were Muslims, but most of the population was Hindu.
Remarkable feature: Detailed miniature paintings.

Indian Ocean

Pacific Ocean

Atlantic cean

What can we learn about Mughal society from the evidence they left behind?

In the last chapter you saw a glimpse of how the Mughals compared to other global powers of the time. Now it is time to find out about who the Mughals really were. The Mughals left behind a lot of evidence of their civilisation. The best evidence is a set of miniature paintings, highly detailed scenes showing life in Mughal India. The originals of the ones in this chapter are only 32cm high – the same height as your ruler!

Historians use evidence to make inferences about the past. An inference is something which is not directly stated in the source, but which you can work out by 'reading between the lines'. On pages 98–99 you are going to make your own inferences about what it was like to live in Mughal India.

Step 1: All the details

We have given you the details and questions around picture A below (labels 1–7) – you just have to make the inferences!

1 In this scene they are building a fortress. Why might they need to build a fortress? What does this tell us about the Mughals?

2 What does the scene suggest about the role of women? Do they have the same position/role as the men?

3 Why is this man holding a stick? What might this tell us about Mughal society?

4 This is Akbar, the emperor. What makes you know he is the ruler? What kind of ruler does he look like? Do you think he is nice to his people or not?

5 These men are holding swords. Why do you think they are necessary? What does this tell us about this society?

6 How are these people being ruled? Are they being ruled by violence or are these people happy to co-operate?

7 The people with the lighter skin are the Mughals who were Muslims. The people with darker skin are Hindus. Do they have the same role/position in this scene? Can you find any exceptions to the rule? What might this tell us?

⬆ A painting of Akbar, the Mughal ruler, directing the construction of a new palace at Fatehphur Sikri. Made for the *Akbarnama*, a chronicle of Akbar's life, *c*.1586.

So far you have been making inferences from evidence, but we have been giving you a lot of help and suggestions. Now we are going to take some of that support away.

Step 2: Some support removed

Look at picture B. Can you make inferences from the following pieces of evidence?

▪ The hawk
▪ The trees in the city
▪ The brightly coloured clothing
▪ The camels.

Using picture B, make inferences to answer the following questions. Make sure you find the evidence which supports your inferences.

▪ How did the Mughals make money?
▪ Why were they so good at war?
▪ Was this a fair society to live in?

Step 3: Go it alone!

Now you have got the idea about how to make an inference it is your turn to make your own.
Come up with your own question that you want to ask about Mughal society and see if you can find details in either picture A or B to infer an answer.

Activity

1 Using all the inferences you have now made, write an answer to the question:

What can we learn about the Mughal society from the evidence they left behind?

It should be really detailed. Remember to use tentative language, such as 'they might have', 'I can infer that'.

2 Pictures A and B are both taken from the *Akbarnama*, a book commissioned by Akbar to record his life. Can we trust what it shows about the Mughals?

3 How different was Mughal society to Tudor society? You could compare picture B to the Bruegel painting (picture A) on pages 22–23. Can you see any similarities?

B

↑ *Ali Quli, Bahadur Khan and Akbar.* A painting of two rebel brothers who are offering their support to Akbar. Made for the *Akbarnama, c.*1586.

Why is Akbar known as 'Akbar the Great'?

On page 99 you compared Mughal society to Tudor society – now you will study how the Mughal rulers compared to the Tudor monarchs.

The Mughal Empire began in 1526, when Babur, a Central Asian ruler, was ousted from his lands and decided to invade India, successfully destroying the opposition at the Battle of Panipat and establishing a new empire. However, his grandson Akbar, who was the third Mughal emperor and ruled from 1542 to 1605, was far more successful. He vastly expanded the Mughal Empire and ruled more than 100 million people (at the same time the Tudor monarchs ruled only 3 million in England). Akbar was given the title 'the Great'. In this chapter you are going to complete a stepped enquiry looking at why Akbar has been given the title 'the Great'.

⬆ Akbar, the third Mughal emperor, ruled from 1542–1605.

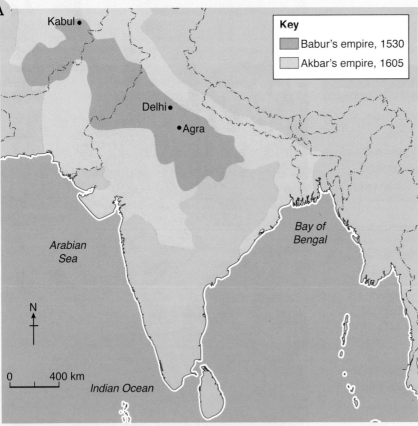

A

Key

■ Babur's empire, 1530

■ Akbar's empire, 1605

⬆ A map of the extent of the Mughal Empire during the reigns of Babur (1526–1530) and his grandson Akbar (1542–1605).

Enquiry Step 1: First evidence – asking questions

Look at map A above. What questions does it make you want to ask about why Akbar was known as 'the Great'?

Our next step is to look at some evidence to find some actual reasons why Akbar was able to expand and control such a vast empire.

B

Akbar and taxation

Akbar created a new taxation system called the dahsala. Tax was set at the rate of one-third of the crops produced. Collectors were lenient towards peasants in years of drought or poor harvest.

C

Akbar on religion

In the past, to our shame, we forced many Hindus to adopt the faith of our ancestors. Now it has become clear to me that in our troubled world … it cannot be wisdom to assert the unique truth of one faith over another.

A quote from the *Akbarnama*.

D

Akbar at his court

It is hard to exaggerate how accessible he makes himself to all who wish audience of him. For he creates an opportunity almost every day for any of the common people or of the nobles to see him and converse with him; and he endeavours to show himself pleasant-spoken and affable, rather than severe, toward all who come to speak with him.

Father Monseratte, a Jesuit (Catholic) priest from Portugal who visited the court of Akbar.

E

⬆ *The Siege of Chittor, 1567,* a painting from the *Akbarnama*, a chronicle of Akbar's life.

Enquiry Step 2: Suggesting an answer

Now it is time to identify some of the reasons that Akbar was so great.

1 Working with a small group, consider the evidence in B–E. For each one, explain how it shows Akbar's greatness. (Note: With picture E remember to use the inference skills you learned on pages 98–99.)

2 Akbar was great with four aspects of ruling – religion, money matters, government and warfare. Can you identify how each piece of evidence above shows this?

3 You will now have a list of 'reasons why Akbar was great'. Which is the most persuasive?

4 What is your initial hypothesis to the question:

   Why is Akbar known as 'Akbar the Great'?

Akbar's problems

On the last page you found out that Akbar was great with religion, money matters, government and warfare. This was because he solved a big problem in each of these areas.

The four problems he faced ruling the Mughal Empire were:

1 ruling a state with different religions – although the Mughals themselves, including Akbar, were Muslims, the majority of the population was Hindu
2 money matters – how to pay for such a vast empire
3 government – how to rule such a vast empire effectively
4 warfare – how to control such a vast empire.

Enquiry Step 3: Developing your answer

1 ▋ Draw a copy of the table below and sort the pieces of evidence B–V from pages 101–105 which give solutions under the relevant problem.
▋ In pairs discuss why each piece of evidence would have helped solve the problem.
▋ Feed your discussion back to the rest of your class.

Problems	Solutions
1 Ruling a state with different religions	
2 How to pay for such a vast empire	
3 How to rule such a vast empire effectively	
4 How to control such a vast empire	

2 Has your initial hypothesis to the question:

Why is Akbar known as 'Akbar the Great'?

changed at all? Do you think he was 'greater' in some areas more than others?

F

Akbar included Hindus in his most high ranking advisors. The Hindu general Man Singh became one of his most trusted advisors.

G

In 1568, once the siege of Chittor was broken (see picture E on page 101), Akbar ordered the massacre of 30,000 men (mostly Hindus) as a sign of his power. By 1570 as a result of this all the chiefs of the Rajasthan region had sworn allegiance to him.

H

In 1581 the slaughter of cows was banned. This was important to Hindus who believed that cows were sacred.

I

In 1564 the *jizya*, a tax on anyone who was not Muslim, was abolished.

J

In 1582 Akbar founded his own religion, Din-e-Ilahi ('the religion of God') which combined the traditions of all the religions of his empire, including Islam and Hinduism.

K

The empire was controlled by a strict system of ranks, the *mansabdari* system (*mansab* literally meaning rank). There were 33 ranks of mansabdars, from the lowest who commanded 10 men, to the highest who commanded 10,000 men. Rank did not directly transfer to your sons but was based on merit and these men helped to control the vast empire.

L

Akbar celebrated Diwali, the Hindu festival of light and Christmas, the Christian festival.

M

This jade terrapin would have taken more than a year to make and is quite large at nearly 50cm long. It was probably designed as an ornament for a pool in the garden at the palace of Akbar's son. It would have cost a very large sum of money and would have been a sign of great wealth and honour to receive such a gift.

N

At the Hall of Private Audience (*Diwan-i-Khas*) Akbar would listen to the advice of great thinkers from many religions while walking on a raised catwalk. His advisors included Hindus, Muslims and Christians. Below you can see the catwalk that Akbar walked around on.

O

Akbar had a young Hindu poet at court, Birbal. He was also a singer and was well known for his wit and intelligence. There are famous folk tales of Birbal outsmarting Akbar's courtiers and even the Emperor himself!

P

Akbar was advised by a group of nine advisors called the *Navaratnas*. These men came from different regions of the Empire.

Q

Akbar's empire is often called a 'gunpowder empire' as they had vast numbers of guns and cannons.

R

After the victory at the Battle of Panipat, Akbar's army took the **war elephants** from his rival Hemu.

S

Akbar built many fortresses in India. The Red Fort in Agra, one of the capitals of the Mughal Empire, is one of the most famous. It was said to have included 500 buildings.

T

Before Akbar, weights and measures varied from region to region, causing great confusion and corruption. Akbar realised the need for a uniform system and so standardised the weights and measurements around the barley corn (*Jau*).

U

There were very few prisons in Mughal India. Instead whippings, public humiliation, banishment or death were set as punishments.

Think

How would you have felt if you had seen an army like the one below approaching?

V

The Mughal army was vast. In 1581 they marched into Kabul with 50,000 cavalry and 500 elephants.

Activity

How does Akbar compare to other leaders of this period?

1 The four problems that Akbar faced were the same ones that the English rulers faced in this period. Copy and complete the table below to see how they compare.

Problems	How did English rulers deal with this problem?	Was this better or worse than Akbar?
1 Religion: Ruling a state with different religions		
2 Money matters: How to raise money for expansion		
3 Government: How to govern effectively		
4 Warfare: How to expand and defend their land		

2 Does this comparison change your opinion about Akbar? Does it make him an even greater leader? Discuss this in pairs and feed back to your class.

Enquiry Step 4: Concluding your enquiry

Over pages 100–105 you have discovered a lot of reasons why Akbar was known as the 'great' and should already have made a hypothesis on this question. From Enquiry Steps 2 and 3 you should have a lot of evidence. Your next step is to decide which evidence is the most important in explaining why Akbar became known as 'the Great'.

Thinking about importance

1   First you need to set criteria. In pairs write down the attributes of a great leader when it comes to:
    ▌ religion ▌ money matters ▌ government ▌ warfare.

2   In Enquiry Step 3 on page 102 you began to think about whether Akbar got his title because he was greater in one area than another. Now you are going to build on this.

    Using the table of solutions to Akbar's problems you made in Enquiry Step 3 on page 102 think about which solutions really did show that Akbar was great, referring back to your criteria. Some evidence will be more important than others. There is not necessarily a right answer here but it is how you argue it.

    Next to each solution in your table add the following codes:

VI = Very important evidence – this definitely showed Akbar was a great leader.

QI = Quite important evidence – this played a fair part in helping Akbar gain his title.

NI = Not important evidence – this only played a tiny part in helping Akbar gain his title.

3   Now it is time to decide on your final answer to the enquiry question. Which of the four big problems which Akbar solved show he was a great leader? Explain why you chose it. Discuss this with a partner or as a class. Was this any different from your original hypothesis?

Communicating your answer

Now you can use the work you have done in Enquiry Steps 1–4 to write an essay in answer to the enquiry question:

Why is Akbar known as 'Akbar the Great'?

Remember that a good essay should contain the following things:

▌ Introduction – this is where you outline the question and grab the attention of the reader.

▌ Paragraphs – this is the main part of the essay where you examine the reasons why Akbar was so great.

▌ Conclusion – this is where you give a judgement about which reason was most important.

▌ Your essay could include some of the following words:

> ▌ Akbar ▌ Mughal ▌ Taxation ▌ Hindu ▌ Muslim ▌ *jizya* ▌ fortress
> ▌ *Din-e-Ilahi* ▌ elephant ▌ *mansabdari* ▌ *dhasala* ▌ *Navaratnas*

Writing paragraphs

A good essay is structured into paragraphs. The four problems and Akbar's solutions will each become a paragraph in your essay.

A good paragraph is like a good burger – both have key ingredients. Without a top bun (opening point), there is nothing to hold the meal together. If you miss out or do not add enough meat (evidence) the burger is tasteless. If you forget the bottom bun (the explanation) the meat (evidence) falls out and is useless! Remember to start with an opening point, back it up with evidence and then explain how this links to the question. Use the sentence starters in the table below to help you.

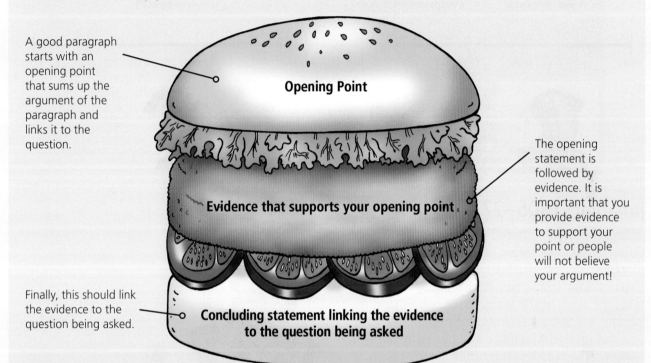

A good paragraph starts with an opening point that sums up the argument of the paragraph and links it to the question.

Opening Point

The opening statement is followed by evidence. It is important that you provide evidence to support your point or people will not believe your argument!

Evidence that supports your opening point

Finally, this should link the evidence to the question being asked.

Concluding statement linking the evidence to the question being asked

Opening point	Evidence	Explanation
One reason Akbar is known as 'the Great' is …	For example … Firstly … Moreover … Furthermore … Secondly … Lastly … Finally …	Therefore … This meant … This led to … This resulted in …

Writing a conclusion

Your conclusion should let the reader know which reason you think was the most important in explaining why Akbar is known as 'the Great'. You have already thought about this in Enquiry Step 4 (page 106).

7

Were the Mughals more successful than the Tudors and Stuarts?

Were later Mughal leaders as successful as Akbar?

After the death of Akbar in 1605 his descendants faced the same problems of ruling a vast empire, yet they tackled these problems in very different ways. In this chapter (pages 108–111) you need to decide if they were as successful as Akbar.

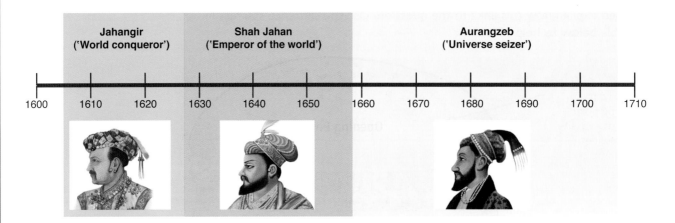

| | Jahangir ('World conqueror') | | Shah Jahan ('Emperor of the world') | | | Aurangzeb ('Universe seizer') | | |

1600 — 1610 — 1620 — 1630 — 1640 — 1650 — 1660 — 1670 — 1680 — 1690 — 1700 — 1710

Jahangir, 1605–27

Jahangir mostly followed in the footsteps of his father, Akbar. In terms of religion he was tolerant towards Hindus, Muslims and Christians. Hindus in particular were given high *mansabdar* rank. Jahangir specifically warned his nobles that they 'should not force Islam on anyone' and the *jizya* (the tax on non-Muslims) was not reintroduced. However, he was less tolerant towards Sikhs. When the fifth of the ten Sikh gurus, Arjun Dev, supported a rebellion, he was executed by being made to sit on a burning hot sheet while boiling hot sand was poured over his body.

Jahangir continued his father's expansion of the Mughal Empire. He consolidated power in North India by defeating the remaining states that Akbar could not defeat, like Mewar. He also began the expansion of the Empire south into the Deccan. However, in 1620 he fell ill and many, including his son Khurram, saw this as an opportunity to take power.

Jahangir was said to be addicted to opium, alcohol and women but, despite his vices, he tried to rule fairly. At Agra he established a 'chain of justice' – an 80 foot long gold chain with 60 bells so that 'the aggrieved might come to this chain and shake it so that its noise might attract my attention'. This was a simple way of ensuring that those with complaints could get attention without any formality. At his court there were many painters and many great artworks were produced.

In 1612 Jahangir signed a treaty with the English **East India Company**. The treaty allowed the English exclusive rights to build ports and factories in the Mughal Empire and in return they promised to provide the Emperor with goods from Europe. This brought the Mughals a lot of money.

A

I desire your Majesty to command your merchants to bring in their ships of all sorts of rarities and rich goods fit for my palace; and that you be pleased to send me your royal letters by every opportunity, that I may rejoice in your health and prosperous affairs; that our friendship may be interchanged and eternal.

A letter from Jahangir to James I, King of England

Shah Jahan, 1627–58

After the death of his father, Khurram took the name Shah Jahan meaning 'Emperor of the world' and his reign is often known as the 'Golden Age' of the Mughals. In his reign there was a great building programme and art and architecture were arguably at their best for the whole rule of the Mughals. Shah Jahan commissioned the building of a city at Delhi, where the new mosque the Jama Masjid, which opened in 1656, could house more than 100,000 worshippers at once.

Unlike Akbar and Jahangir, Shah Jahan was a very strict Muslim and began changing the rules around religion. In 1633 he began to impose some parts of **Shari'ah law** (Islamic law) which banned the repair of Christian churches or Hindu temples and even ordered the destruction of some new Hindu temples. He celebrated Islamic festivals with great pomp and ceremony.

In his reign there was a great famine in the Deccan region between the years 1630 and 1632. Shah Jahan donated only 5000 rupees a week to aid his people. At the same time he had the Peacock Throne constructed for himself which cost billions of rupees. The chair took seven years to build, cost twice as much as the Taj Mahal and was made of solid gold, precious stones and pearls. To pay for projects like this Shah Jahan increased the amount of tax from one-third of crop produce to one-half of crop produce.

The Mughal Empire continued to expand under Shah Jahan. In 1638 he captured the city of Kandahar (in modern day Afghanistan) which had proved tricky to conquer for the Mughals – although it was later recaptured by the **Persians**. To rule the Empire Shah Jahan still used the *mansabdari* system of rank but he reduced the number of those with power to give him more of an elite ruling class.

B

⬆ The Taj Mahal. Upon the death of his wife Mumtaz Mahal, Shah Jahan ordered the building of a great mausoleum to commemorate her – the Taj Mahal is now known as one of the most beautiful buildings in the world. Started in 1631, it supposedly took 20,000 workers 20 years to build it.

Activity

1 Is 'Golden Age' an appropriate term for Shah Jahan's reign? Answer this question referring to picture B.
2 Discuss the following question in a small group, then share your ideas as a class:
Shah Jahan and Jahangir dealt with things very differently to Akbar. Does this make them less successful than Akbar? Remember to think about how successful they were in terms of religion, money matters, government and warfare.

Aurangzeb, 1658–1707

As Shah Jahan fell ill in the 1650s, a war of succession began over who should be the ruler. Dara Shikoh, the eldest son, wanted to create a society where Muslims and Hindus could live together but Aurangzeb, the third son, wanted to make a more Muslim focused country. In 1658 Aurangzeb beat his brother in battle and the following year paraded him into Delhi on the back of a filthy elephant where he was executed in front of his own son by four of Aurangzeb's henchmen.

Aurangzeb is a controversial figure. He is arguably the most effective Mughal leader as the Empire extended the furthest under his rule. However, his policies towards Hindus and Sikhs have left him hated to this day by some.

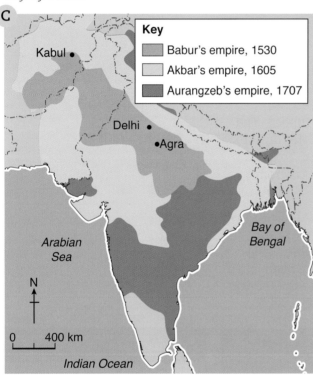

C

Key
- Babur's empire, 1530
- Akbar's empire, 1605
- Aurangzeb's empire, 1707

Kabul

Delhi

Agra

Arabian Sea

Bay of Bengal

N

0   400 km

Indian Ocean

⬆ A map showing the expansion of the Mughal Empire under Aurangzeb.

D

Your subjects are trampled underfoot; every province of your empire is impoverished; depopulation spreads and difficulties accumulate ... If your majesty places any faith in those holy books, you will there be instructed that God is the God of all mankind, not the God of Muslims alone.

An anonymous letter of complaint sent to Aurangzeb.

Aurangzeb and religion

Aurangzeb's religious policies aimed to create an Islamic state. He followed Shari'ah law closely and banned alcohol, gambling and some writers even claim he banned music. He created *muhtasibs* who were 'censors of public morals' and travelled the Empire to make sure that Islamic rule was obeyed. Anyone caught going against this, for example, gambling or drinking heavily, was severely punished.

He was not tolerant of other religions and Hindus and Sikhs suffered. In 1668 Hindu religious fairs were outlawed and no new temple permits were given. Some key Hindu temples were destroyed including Kesava Deo, one of the most important Hindu temples – a Muslim mosque was built on its site. The number of temples that were destroyed is much debated, with figures varying from 80 to 60,000, although some modern historians now believe that Aurangzeb was not trying to destroy religious sites, but to impose his control over areas which might rebel against him.

In 1679 the unpopular non-Muslim tax, the *jizya* was re-imposed. When people protested they were crushed by imperial elephants. The Sikhs, who had supported Aurangzeb's brother Dara during the war of succession, were seen as the enemy and the ninth Sikh guru, Guru Tegh Bahadur, was executed. As a result many Sikhs took the name Singh, meaning 'lion', to show their opposition to Aurangzeb.

> **Think**
>
> Read letter D. How do you think Aurangzeb would have reacted to a letter like this?

Aurangzeb and empire

As you can see in map C on page 110 the Mughal Empire expanded greatly under Aurangzeb. This meant he was able to claim a huge amount of tax with an annual income of over £38 million in 1690, a colossal sum at the time, enabling him to improve his army with more cannons. However, with such a large empire he faced a lot of rebellions, including from his own sons, and his fight to keep the Deccan region in the south cost an estimated 100,000 lives a year.

The English East India Company continued to trade in India and relations between the Mughals and the company remained friendly on the whole. However in 1685, war broke out between the two over trading negotiations. In 1689 Aurangzeb's forces defeated the English allowing him to renegotiate better terms and the English continued to trade with India.

Think

Read extract E below. Is Stanley Wolpert's summary of Shah Jahan applicable to Aurangzeb too?

 E

The formal gardens, marble mausoleums and Persian miniatures were as nectar squeezed from a sub-continent crushed into obedience, milled [stripped] of its riches by the few.

Stanley Wolpert, an expert historian on India, writing about Shah Jahan in 1977.

Activity

1 Now we have looked at the later Mughal leaders it is time to consider if they were as successful as Akbar.

Copy the table below and for each category give each leader a score out of ten (ten being very good) at how effective they were with dealing with each aspect.

Leader	Religion	Money matters	Government	Warfare/ Empire
Akbar				
Jahangir				
Shah Jahan				
Aurangzeb				

2 Now you should have a really good idea about which leader you think was the most successful. Below are two very different ways for you present your answer to the question:

Were later Mughal leaders as successful as Akbar?

No matter which option you choose remember that you must use specific evidence from pages 100–111 in your answer.

OPTION A: A written answer

Explain why the leader with the largest score was the best.

OPTION B: A miniature painting

As you have already discovered, the Mughals made very famous miniature paintings. Many of these were allegorical, telling a story. Your challenge is to present the answer to this question in the form of a picture. For example, you might have a pyramid of the best leaders with the best on top. Remember to include as many historical details from these pages as you can!

7

Were the Mughals more successful than the Tudors and Stuarts?

Were the Mughals more successful than the Tudors and Stuarts?

The bell rings – 'ding-ding'. The fight begins. Akbar the Great attacks first with a flurry of blows. Henry VIII coming from the opposite corner takes the punches well and returns an upper cut knocking his Mughal opponent temporarily off his feet.

This would never actually happen! But let's imagine if it did – who would win? The Mughals or the Tudors and Stuarts? This section of the book so far has looked at how successful the Mughals were in ruling their empire but now you need to compare them to the Tudors and Stuarts who you learned about in the rest of the book.

Activity

⊺ As a class split into two groups – one to champion the Mughals, the other to champion the Tudors and Stuarts. Debate who was the most successful in ruling their country!

Hold your debate like a boxing match, in four rounds, each with a different focus, taking turns to present your arguments:

⊟ What evidence shows how your side (either the Mughals or the Tudors and Stuarts) were the best?

⊟ What evidence will your opponent use to attack you, and how might you best defend yourself against them?

⊟ What evidence delivers that 'knockout blow' which *proves* your side was clearly the most successful? For each round we have suggested where you might look to find that decisive piece of evidence.

Remember you must only argue why *your group* was the most successful – stick to it and allow as many people as possible to speak.

Round 1: Religion

The Mughals had to rule a Hindu population while being Muslim themselves whereas the Tudors and Stuarts had to cope with the conflict between Protestants and Catholics. Who dealt with their religious problem more successfully?

Mughals: Look at pages 102–111.

Tudors and Stuarts: Look at Section 4, pages 40–63.

Round 2: Money matters

Running a country or empire costs a lot of money. One of the most important jobs for a successful ruler is working out how to pay for this. Who did this better – the Mughals or the Tudors and Stuarts? You will need to think very carefully about what 'success' in money matters means. For example, is it acceptable to tax your people unfairly? Is spending lots good or bad?

Mughals: Look at pages 102–111.

Tudors and Stuarts: Look at pages 64–65, 82–83 and 92.

Round 3: Government

Governing in this early modern period was a tricky business and both the Mughals and the Tudors and Stuarts realised this. Each leader did it in a different way. Was it good to rule on your own or better to share power with the people? Were rebellions or civil wars a sign of weakness or a sign that people were jealous of your power?

Mughals: Look at pages 102–111.

Tudors and Stuarts: Look at Section 6, pages 76–95.

Round 4: Warfare

With the widespread use of gunpowder and in a time of expanding empires, warfare was fundamental to the success of a leader in this era. Both the Mughals and the Tudors and Stuarts greatly expanded their empires, moving beyond the borders of their original land. Both groups showed great skill in fighting battles, from the Spanish Armada to the Siege of Chittor. Who do you think was the best?

Mughals: Look at pages 102–111.

Tudors and Stuarts: Look at Section 9, pages 128–141.

Activity

2 Working on your own, write notes on the enquiry question:

Were the Mughals more successful than the Tudors and Stuarts?

▍ Put a sub-title: 'Religion'. Drawing on your discussion work above, write a paragraph describing what the Mughal emperors did, and what the Tudor and Stuart rulers did, and then explaining who you think was the more successful in that area.

▍ Repeat this for the categories: money matters, government and warfare.

▍ Finally, write a conclusion, explaining which you thought was the more successful, and why.

How united was the United Kingdom in 1745?

Historians have to answer many different kinds of question. The easiest are the factual 'knowledge' questions, such as 'When did Henry VIII become king?'

Then there are harder questions, with not one answer but a range of possible answers. 'Causation' questions are like this – to answer to the question 'Why did the Civil War break out in 1642?' you need to explain a number of different factors, of varying importance.

Answering 'How far ...?' questions

The hardest kind of question (and the one which historians usually end up trying to answer) is the 'How far ...?' question.

Many historical questions usually end up being about 'how far', even if they do not use the actual words. For example, you probably ended Section 3 ('Did life get better, 1509–1745?') with an answer along the lines of: 'To some degree yes ... in other ways no'.

What makes these 'How far ...?' questions so hard is that there are no units of measurement which will allow you to measure 'How united was the United Kingdom in 1745?' in the way you could, for example, measure 'How loud?' in decibels or 'Are we nearly there yet?' in miles-to-go.

This section asks:

How united was the United Kingdom in 1745?

You will study each of the 'home nations' – Wales, Ireland and Scotland – in turn, assessing the evidence for and against. Then we will show you how to answer a 'How far ...?' question like this.

How angry?

BOILING MAD

ENRAGED

FURIOUS

FRUSTRATED

ANNOYED

Activity

1   Imagine a referee has wrongly awarded a penalty. How would you start to measure: 'How angry was the football manager?' If you discuss as a class how you might go about answering such a question, it will help you understand how to tackle a historical 'How far ...?' question.

2   What might be the signs that a country was incredibly disunited and about to fall apart? Can you think of any examples of countries where this has happened/is happening?

3   What might be the signs that a country is very united? Can you think of any examples of countries which are very united?

Case Study 1: How united were England and Wales by 1745?

England had conquered Wales in the thirteenth century, and the last Welsh rebellion had been in 1400. In 1536, Wales was united administratively with England – but how 'united' were the two peoples? This enquiry asks you to decide.

Henry VIII wanted greater control over Wales. The Acts of Union of 1536 and 1543 made the laws of Wales the same as the laws of England, and openly stated that their aim was to wipe out the 'sinister' Welsh customs.

Were the Welsh gentry traitors?

The Welsh 'gentry' – about twenty families – were happy to support the Union. They became MPs, sent their sons to Oxford University, sat as Justices of the Peace and imposed English laws on their Welsh neighbours … English laws which kept them in their power and wealth.

About half a million people lived in Wales in 1745; a third of them 'abject poor', living in one-roomed hovels without windows or chimneys. Many became soldiers in the British army, others emigrated to the English colonies in North America or the West Indies.

As only English was used in the courts and government, eventually only the poorest Welsh people spoke Welsh. In 1588, however, William Morgan translated the Bible into Welsh, and in 1715, the Welsh poet Lewis Morris founded the Honourable and Loyal Society of Antient Britons. Its members celebrated St David's Day, and worked to preserve Welsh culture.

Activity

1 The Welsh historian Owen Edwards (1922) declared the Welsh in this period 'a law-abiding and loyal people' and called the Early Modern Era 'two centuries of sleep' for Welsh nationalism. Working with a partner or in a small group, find FOUR pieces of evidence which suggest that the Welsh were happily united with England by 1745.

2 Find TWO pieces of evidence which suggest that not all the Welsh were prepared to be totally absorbed into English society and culture. Write your six pieces of evidence – for and against – onto six cards.

3 Share your findings as a whole class. How reconciled to English rule were the Welsh in 1745?

Case Study 2: How united were England and Ireland by 1745?

England had conquered Ireland in 1171, but by the end of the Middle Ages English influence had shrunk to a small area around Dublin called 'the Pale'. During the Early Modern Era, England increased its control over Ireland – but how 'united' were the two peoples? This enquiry will ask you to decide.

We are going to begin by studying a famous proposal by the **satirist** Jonathan Swift, Dean of Dublin Cathedral in Ireland (who is famous for writing *Gulliver's Travels*).

A

How to solve poverty in Ireland

It is a melancholy object to those, who walk through this great town, or travel in the country, when they see the streets, the roads and cabbin-doors crowded with beggars of the female sex, followed by three, four, or six children, all in rags, and importuning every passenger for alms …

The question therefore is, How this number shall be reared, and provided for? For we can neither employ them in handicraft or agriculture; we neither build houses, nor cultivate land: they can very seldom pick up a livelihood by stealing till they arrive at six years old …

I shall now therefore humbly propose my own thoughts, which I hope will not be liable to the least objection. I have been assured … that a young healthy child well nursed, is, at a year old, a most delicious nourishing and wholesome food, whether stewed, roasted, baked, or boiled … I grant this food will be somewhat dear, and therefore very proper for landlords, who, as they have already devoured most of the parents, seem to have the best title to the children …

Therefore let no man talk to me of other expedients: Of taxing our absentee landlords: Of using neither cloathes, nor houshold furniture, except what is of our own manufacture … Of teaching landlords to have at least one degree of mercy towards their tenants.

But, as to my self, having been wearied out for many years with offering vain, idle, visionary thoughts, and at length utterly despairing of success, I fortunately fell upon this proposal, which, as it is wholly new, of no expence and little trouble, full in our own power, and whereby we can incur no danger in disobliging England. For this kind of commodity will not bear exportation … although perhaps I could name a country, which would be glad to eat up our whole nation.

Jonathan Swift, *A Modest Proposal for Preventing the Children of Poor People From Being a Burthen to Their Parents or Country* (1729)

Enquiry Step 1: First evidence – asking questions

1 Read extract A out loud: did Swift mean what he was proposing? If not, why did he write it?

2 Working in a small group discuss: If extract A was all you knew about Ireland in this period, what conclusions might you form about Ireland, especially:
   a) What were FOUR problems facing Ireland at this time?
   b) What were the TWO main causes of those problems (whom did Swift most blame)?

3 What questions do you want to ask about this source and the situation in Ireland in 1729?

England and Ireland, 1509–1745

How did you answer question 2b on page 116? It is difficult not to come to the conclusion that Swift fairly much blamed England for Ireland's problems! It is time to find out about the relationship between England and Ireland in the Early Modern Era. The diagram below lists the key events of the years 1509–1745 – like a game of 'Hangman' which Ireland lost.

4
In 1649, Cromwell brutally conquered Ireland; at Drogheda and Wexford his men massacred the defenders. During the **Interregnum**, 12,000 Irish were sold into slavery.

5
After 1651, all trade to and from Ireland had to be carried in English ships. Irish farmers were forbidden to export wool or cattle. Huge taxes ruined Irish industries.

3
After 1609, land was confiscated from the Irish Catholics and given to Protestant Scottish and English colonists – by 1703, Irish Catholics owned less than 15 per cent of the land in Ireland. Many landowners were 'absentee landlords' who lived in England.

6
The **Jacobite** Rebellion of 1689 was finally defeated by William of Orange at the Battle of the Boyne (1690); the victorious Protestants killed the wounded Irish Catholics.

7
The period after 1693 is known as 'the Protestant Ascendency'. Catholics were hit by penal laws – they could not own a horse worth more than £5, marry a Protestant, teach, vote or hold public office. Catholic priests were forced to leave Ireland.

2
In the reign of Elizabeth I, there were rebellions in 1562–67, 1569–73, 1579–80 and 1594–1603; they were all brutally suppressed.

1
In 1541, Henry VIII declared himself king of Ireland and imposed English laws.

8
In 1740–41, the Great Frost (the last cold spell of the 'Little Ice Age' – see page 31) coupled with a potato fungus, caused a famine known as 'the year of slaughter' – a third of a million people (one in eight of the population) died.

Enquiry Step 2: Suggesting an answer

1 Working in a small group, study the boxes around the hangman, and then discuss what these tell you about the relationship between England and Ireland in the Early Modern Era. Suggest SIX reasons the Irish had cause to hate the English.

2 There was no rebellion in Ireland in the years 1691–1745; does this suggest that the Irish were happy with English rule by 1745? What else might it suggest?

Interpretations of Irish history

For many years, there was not one history of Ireland, but three, each written from a different viewpoint:

- The Nationalist history of Ireland was one of 'a small nation that endured famines and massacres in endless succession, but never surrendered her soul'. This interpretation of Irish history blamed the English as invaders, oppressors, racists and religious persecutors, and hated Cromwell and William of Orange.
- The Loyalist history of Ireland was of a minority Protestant community, resisting the forces of evil which surrounded them. This history still celebrates William's victory in 1690, and calls itself 'Orange'.
- The English history of Ireland portrayed the Irish as 'backward' and 'troublesome'. It ignored or tried to explain away the darker side of English rule (such as the Drogheda massacre).

Most modern historians argue that none of these 'myths' are true. They say that English 'brutality' was simply how all rebellions were quelled in those days. Equally, they suggest that Irish Catholics were not much worse treated than poor English people in the eighteenth century.

⬆ An image from *An Illustrated History of Ireland*, written in 1868 by Mary Frances Cusack, an Irish Catholic nun.

English Proteftantes ſtriped naked & turned into the mountaines in the froſt, & ſnowe, whereof many hundreds are periſhed to death, & many lyinge dead in diches & Sauages upbraided them ſaynge now are ye wilde Iriſch as well as wee.

⬆ A picture from *The Teares of Ireland*, a book about a Catholic rebellion published in 1641.

⬆ A cartoon from *Punch* magazine, 1881: Britannia, holding a sword, protects Ireland against 'Anarchy' (a violent Irish peasant).

Enquiry Step 3: Developing your answer

Working as a whole class:

▋ Match the three pictures, B–D, to the three different 'histories' of Ireland: Nationalist; Loyalist; English.

▋ The opinion you formed on page 117 (about whether the Irish were happy with English rule in 1745) was based on a very 'nationalist' presentation of the facts. Has the information on page 118 altered your judgement?

F

⬆ *The Fermanagh Man-Eater.* There are many pictures of impossible mythical monsters dating from the Middle Ages. However, this picture – by the German engraver Elias Baeck – of a creature from Fermanagh in Northern Ireland, is dated 1720!

E

The people of Connaught in 1709

I did not see all this way three living creatures, not one house or ditch, not one bit of corn, nor even, I might say, a bit of land, for stones: in short nothing appear'd but stones and sea, nor could I conceive an inhabited country so destitute of all signs of people and art as this is. Yet here, I hear, live multitudes of barbarous uncivilized Irish after their old fashions, who are here one and all in ye defence of any of their own or even other rogues that fly to them, against the laws of Ireland, so that here is the assylum, here are committed the most barbarous murders after shipracks, and all manner of roguerys protected, that the Sheriffs of this county scarce dare appear.

An eyewitness description of Connaught by the traveller Samuel Molyneaux – a gentleman-scientist who went to Dublin University and served as an MP on both the English and Irish Parliaments. Molyneaux was travelling round visiting different loyalist landlords.

In the years 1711–13, night raiders called 'the Houghers' terrorised Connaught, killing the landlords' cattle. The local peasants sang ballads praising them, and local Catholic priests said prayers for their success.

Enquiry Step 4: Concluding your enquiry

1 Study extract E.
   ▋ Why are there no sources from Irish peasants describing how angry they were?
   ▋ Nobody knows what caused the Houghers' raids, because there are no remaining written records. Using extract E, suggest why they did what they did.

2 What does evidence E and F tell us about how the English felt about the Irish?

3 Working with a partner or in a small group, review the evidence you have collected from pages 116–119 and choose the FOUR best pieces of evidence that the people of Ireland were hostile to English rule.

4 Now revisit pages 116–119 again, and find TWO pieces of evidence which show that some people in Ireland accepted and welcomed English rule. Write your six pieces of evidence – for and against – onto cards.

5 Share your findings as a whole class: how reconciled to English rule were the Irish in 1745?

Case Study 3: How united were England and Scotland by 1745?

Scotland and England were continually at war during the Middle Ages, and Edward I had tried but failed to conquer Scotland. During the Early Modern Era, however, England gradually increased its control and in 1707 the two countries were united – but how 'united' were the two peoples?

In 1791, the famous Scottish poet Robert Burns wrote this poem, still furious at the decision in the Scottish Parliament (in 1707) to agree the Act of Union with England and to form the United Kingdom:

⬆ The highlands and lowlands of Scotland.

A

Such a Parcel of Rogues in a Nation

Fareweel to a' our Scottish fame,
Fareweel our ancient glory;
Fareweel ev'n to the Scottish name,
Sae fam'd in martial story.
Now Sark rins over Solway sands,
An' Tweed rins to the ocean,
To mark where England's province stands –
Such a parcel of rogues in a nation!

The Sark and the Tweed are the rivers which marked the former border of Scotland.

What force or guile could not subdue,
Thro' many warlike ages,
Is wrought now by a coward few,
For hireling traitor's wages.
The English steel we could disdain,
Secure in valour's station;
But English gold has been our bane –
Such a parcel of rogues in a nation!

'Bane' means ruin.

O would, or I had seen the day
That Treason thus could sell us,
My auld grey head had lain in clay,
Wi' Bruce and loyal Wallace!
But pith and power, till my last hour,
I'll mak this declaration;
We're bought and sold for English gold –
Such a parcel of rogues in a nation!

Bruce and Wallace were Scottish heroes who fought England in the Middle Ages.

'Pith' means effort.

Enquiry Step 1: First evidence – asking questions

1 Working in a small group, read poem A out loud, and discuss what it means.

2 What questions do you want to ask about this poem to understand what was going on?

England and Scotland, 1509–1745

How did you answer question 2 on page 120? One sensible
starting point as you try to understand what was going on would
be to study a 'timeline' of events 1509–1745.

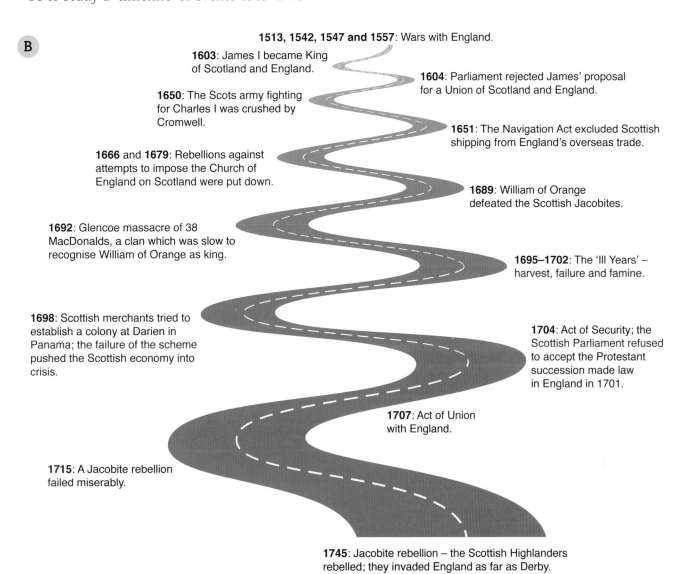

B

1513, 1542, 1547 and 1557: Wars with England.

1603: James I became King of Scotland and England.

1604: Parliament rejected James' proposal for a Union of Scotland and England.

1650: The Scots army fighting for Charles I was crushed by Cromwell.

1651: The Navigation Act excluded Scottish shipping from England's overseas trade.

1666 and **1679**: Rebellions against attempts to impose the Church of England on Scotland were put down.

1689: William of Orange defeated the Scottish Jacobites.

1692: Glencoe massacre of 38 MacDonalds, a clan which was slow to recognise William of Orange as king.

1695–1702: The 'Ill Years' – harvest, failure and famine.

1698: Scottish merchants tried to establish a colony at Darien in Panama; the failure of the scheme pushed the Scottish economy into crisis.

1704: Act of Security; the Scottish Parliament refused to accept the Protestant succession made law in England in 1701.

1707: Act of Union with England.

1715: A Jacobite rebellion failed miserably.

1745: Jacobite rebellion – the Scottish Highlanders rebelled; they invaded England as far as Derby.

⬆ The long and winding road: Anglo-Scottish relations, 1509 to 1745.

Enquiry Step 2: Suggesting an answer

1 Working in a small group, discuss what the long and winding road timeline B above tells you about the relationship between England and Scotland in the Early Modern Era. Suggest FIVE reasons the Scots had cause to hate the English.

2 There were three acts of resistance to England's domination of Scotland in the years 1692–1745, but none in Ireland; does this suggest that the Scottish were even less happy with English rule than the Irish? What else might it suggest?

The Act of Union

Until 1707, Scotland was independent from England, although the two countries shared the same monarch after 1603. Many Scots hated the English, blaming them not only for William of Orange's campaign of 1689 and the Glencoe Massacre, but also for failing to help during the 'Ill Years' of famine and the failure of the colony at Darien.

And when the English Parliament passed the Act of Settlement, stating that the crown would pass to George, ruler of Hanover (see page 92), the Scottish Parliament passed the Act of Security (1704) stating that – when Anne died – they would choose their own monarch. In England, the politicians decided that it was union or war, and asked for negotiations for a union.

The debate about negotiating a union with England was held in the Scottish Parliament without warning at the end of a session when many Scottish MPs had gone home. Scottish MPs who supported the union were accused of being bribed.

Nevertheless, in 1707 the Scots accepted the union – it was the beginning of the United Kingdom. The union was a good deal for the Scots, who paid lower taxes, and became part of England's **Industrial Revolution.**

By the nineteenth century, Scotland was a contented partner within the United Kingdom. But how did they feel about the union in 1745?

C

I see a free and independent kingdom delivering up that which all the world hath been fighting for since the days of **Nimrod** … I think I see a petty English taxman receive more homage and respect than what was paid formerly [to the noble peerage of Scotland] … Good God! Is this an entire surrender?

Lord Belhaven, speaking in 1706; at this point, he asked for a moment to weep.

D

⬆ The flower that was named 'Sweet William' in England was called 'Stinking Billy' in Scotland.

E

In 1726–37, the English general George Wade built more than 250 miles of military roads in Scotland, with four army garrisons, and a naval warship on Loch Ness, as a defence against the Highlanders.

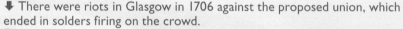

⬇ There were riots in Glasgow in 1706 against the proposed union, which ended in solders firing on the crowd.

F

G

The 1708 invasion

In 1708, there was an attempted Jacobite invasion of Scotland; 30,000 men were supposed to be ready to rise in support of James, the son of the Stuart king James II who had been deposed in 1689. But in the event nothing happened. The French fleet was defeated and nobody rebelled.

This British coin celebrated the victory. On the left, rebels are being imprisoned in the Tower of London, on the right the French fleet is defeated. The Latin inscriptions mean: 'Who can freely attack us when we are united' and 'James fails to return to Scotland; the French fleet is put to flight'.

In the centre an English rose and the Scottish thistle intertwine.

H

Secret plots

The Jacobites plotted in secret. They developed many symbols and signs. When they toasted the king, they held their glasses over the water jug, so they were toasting 'the king over the water'.

Other Jacobite symbols included:

- a white rose (as shown in this painting of a Jacobite lady)
- the butterfly (signifying their hope to burst into rebellion like a butterfly from a chrysalis)
- an oak leaf (a symbol of strength and safety)
- the sunflower (a symbol of loyalty).

I

The 1715 Rebellion

> The Union has begun our nation's ruin and will, in all probability, in a short time complete it … Whoever had been king, when my nation's interest came to compete with theirs, I would have been their enemy because my principles oblige me to prefer my country's interest even before my own.

A letter from William Scott of Ancrum, explaining to his brother why he joined the rebellion of 1715.

The Highlanders rose, and a Jacobite army of 4000 defeated the government's army at Sheriffmuir (near Perth). However, despite their victory, the Highlanders retreated. Further south, an attempt by only 80 Jacobites to capture Edinburgh Castle was a disaster, and the rebellion fizzled out.

Enquiry Step 3: Developing your answer

1 Working as a whole class:
   - Find FOUR reasons in evidence C and I on pages 122–123 why some Scots opposed the Union.
   - Discuss how the information on pages 122–123 helps us to better understand Robert Burns' poem *Such a Parcel of Rogues in a Nation* on page 120.

2 Can you see any evidence that might lead you to conclude that the opposition to the union was not as great as the Jacobites hoped?

The 'Forty-Five' Rebellion

By 1745, the Jacobites – believing that Scotland was seething with discontent – judged the time right to rebel again; it gives us an insight into how united England and Scotland were.

Think

What does picture J tell us about how Londoners felt about the Scots?

Bonnie Prince Charlie – the Jacobite claimant to the throne – landed in the Hebrides in July 1745.

An army of 5000 Highlanders flocked to him and defeated an English army at Prestonpans in four minutes.

The Scots invaded England. There was panic in London, but no Englishmen joined the rebellion.

At Derby, the Scots refused to go any further, and retreated. The Scots were finally defeated at the Battle of Culloden in 1746.

The English killed the wounded where they lay.

All the Scottish nobles who had taken part were executed; 1000 prisoners were **transported**.

Charles was hunted by the English but escaped; no one betrayed him. The English destroyed the traditions and culture of the rebellious Highlanders – for example, forbidding them to wear tartan or play the bagpipes.

J

⬆ This engraving – *Sawney in the Boghouse* – was published in London in 1745. It shows a Scotsman struggling to understand how to use a toilet. (Sawney Bean was a legendary sixteenth-century Scottish mass-murderer and cannibal.)

Enquiry Step 4: Concluding your enquiry

1 Working with a partner or in a small group, review the evidence you have collected from pages 120–124 and choose the FOUR best pieces of evidence that the people of Scotland were hostile to English rule.

2 Now revisit pages 120–124 again, and find TWO pieces of evidence which show that not everybody in Scotland hated English rule. Write your six pieces of evidence – for and against – onto cards.

3 Share your findings as a whole class: how reconciled to union with England were the Scots in 1745?

Pulling it all together: How united was the United Kingdom in 1745?

This section (pages 114–124) has studied the development of the United Kingdom from 1509 to 1745, and has looked, in turn, at how united Wales, Ireland and Scotland were with England by the end of the period.

So now is the time to pull all your ideas together, and to come to a conclusion about how united the United Kingdom was by 1745.

Activity

1 Working as a whole class, review your learning about Wales, Ireland and Scotland. For each nation, you will have SIX cards relating to how the people of the home countries felt about the English – Wales mainly for, Ireland and Scotland mainly against.
2 Revisit the sets of cards, and for each nation, discuss how united they were with England by 1745. For each nation – Welsh, Irish and Scottish – come up with a sentence which sums up their relationship with England. Include quantity-words such as 'overwhelmingly', 'to a small extent', 'intensely' and so on.
3 Draw a large picture of a pair of scales like the one opposite.
   ▌ Onto one pan, put all the cards which show evidence of unity.
   ▌ Onto the other pan, put all the cards which show evidence of disunity.
   As you place each card, read it out loud, and discuss and explain as a class how it shows unity/disunity.

4 Finally, working on your own, write an essay about how united the United Kingdom was in 1745.

   ▌ Start by writing:

   On the one hand, there is some evidence that the United Kingdom was fairly well-united in 1745.

   Then write a paragraph describing and explaining all the evidence of unity you have found (more in Wales than in Ireland and Scotland).

   ▌ Next, write:

   On the other hand, there is a lot of evidence that the nations of the United Kingdom were far from being united in 1745.

   Then write a paragraph describing and explaining all the evidence of disunity and hatred you have found.

   ▌ Finally, write a conclusion.
   a) Start by using your sentences from question 2 to sum up England's relationship with the three nations,
   b) Then write a final section where you deliver your judgement about how united the United Kingdom was overall. A good essay will provide the key facts and explanations which prove that your judgement is correct.

125

Did Britannia rule the waves in 1745?

When you studied the Middle Ages, you saw that the nature of warfare changed – from raids and local wars before 1066, to religious crusades and wars to build dynastic empires, 1066–1509.

Things also changed during the Early Modern Years. The countries of Europe fought bitter wars of religion – for example, the Thirty Years War (1618–48) which devastated most of Germany.

Also, countries ceased to be merely the possessions of a royal family. They developed a sense of identity and became 'nations', and fought each other for power, trade and empire.

Towards the end of the seventeenth century, the rulers of the time formed leagues and alliances, and tried to write treaties which would prevent war. However, they failed: the eighteenth century was a time of almost continuous wars.

A

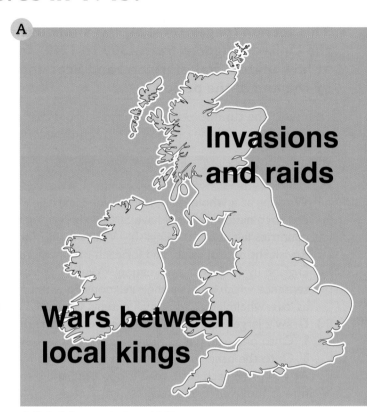

Invasions and raids

Wars between local kings

⬆ Britain's wars before 1066

B

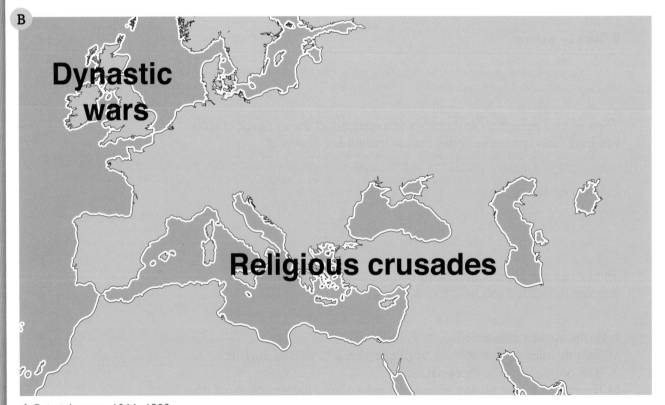

Dynastic wars

Religious crusades

⬆ Britain's wars, 1066–1509

During most of the Early Modern Era, English interventions in European wars tended to be unsuccessful; after 1600 the English concentrated increasingly on trade, the navy and its overseas empire. By 1745, Britain had built up a scattered empire of small colonies, trading posts and naval bases – which historians recognise as the beginnings of the British Empire.

By the end of the nineteenth century, that Empire ruled 458 million people and covered a quarter of the world's land area.

But how powerful was the emerging British Empire in the Early Modern Era? In this section you will be exploring the question:

Did Britannia rule the waves in 1745?

Activity

1 What are wars fought about nowadays? Using maps A–C on pages 126–127, construct a case that international relations became 'modern' in the Early Modern Era.
2 The areas coloured red on map C show the extent of England's colonial empire and trading posts in 1745. Thinking back to your work on the world powers of the sixteenth century (on pages 96–97), would you call England 'a world power' in 1745?

C

Britain's international relations in 1745

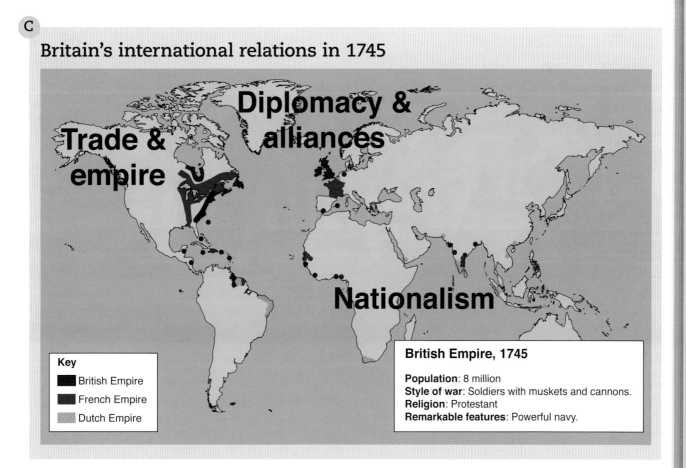

Trade & empire

Diplomacy & alliances

Nationalism

Key
- British Empire
- French Empire
- Dutch Empire

British Empire, 1745

Population: 8 million
Style of war: Soldiers with muskets and cannons.
Religion: Protestant
Remarkable features: Powerful navy.

How 'glorious' was the defeat of the Armada?

When I (Mr Clare) was a small child and was sent to bed, I used to sneak a torch and read under the bedclothes. I used to read a children's encyclopaedia from the 1930s – *Newnes' Pictorial Knowledge* – and volume 2 gave me my love of history.

This section asks the question:

Did Britannia rule the waves in 1745?

My *Newnes' Pictorial Knowledge* had no doubt about the answer to that question. It was 'YES!' And not only was the answer 'yes' in 1745 but – looking back further into history – it saw Great Britain's greatness stretching far back into the reign of Elizabeth.

This chapter will help you to come to your own conclusions by studying what *Newnes' Pictorial Knowledge* held to be Elizabeth's greatest victory – the defeat of the Armada:

> **Enquiry Step 1: First evidence – asking questions**
>
> 1 Look carefully at picture A. If you had no other knowledge, what would you infer about the Armada from picture A alone?
>
> 2 What questions do you want to ask about this picture and this event?

A

⬆ 'THE ARMADA IS IN SIGHT!' *Newnes' Pictorial Knowledge* illustrated its story of the Armada with this 1880 painting. The caption read: 'In this realistic masterpiece Seymour Lucas, HA., depicted the scene on a sunny afternoon in July, 1588, when an officer brought the news of the approach of the Spanish Armada invasion fleet. At the time Sir Francis Drake, the first Englishman to sail in one voyage round the world, was playing on the bowling green of the Hoe at Plymouth with a group of captains. Hearing that the enemy was in sight, Drake laughingly declared that there was plenty of time to win the game and beat the Spaniards too!'

B

For thirty years

Elizabeth set to work to make her subjects happy and prosperous, to raise England to a high place among the nations of Europe, and to lay the foundations of a great empire.

The enmity of the Pope and of the two great supporters of the Roman Catholic Church – Spain and France – forced her into the position of being the chief upholder of the Reformation, both in England and abroad. More and more the struggle narrowed down to a contest between Spain and England. The conflict between these two countries was made worse by the commercial rivalry that gradually sprang up between them. The stories that were told of the Spanish colonies in America, and of the wonderful treasures that were to be had there, fired the imagination and roused the ambition of the gallant English sailors of that time. At first they went out to see these new lands, to try to trade with them, and to discover others like them. But quite often these expeditions ended in bloodshed and the sinking or burning of ships, and that led in turn to more fighting and bitter hatred.

Sir Francis Drake

Of all the great adventurers who wrought such havoc on 'the Spanish Main,' none is so famous as Sir Francis Drake. On two occasions, he led little fleets of ships across the Atlantic; and there, by attacking and plundering Spanish vessels and cities, won for himself the name of 'The Dragon'.

Knowing that Philip was preparing a great navy with which to invade England, Elizabeth sent Drake to do what he could against it, and the fearless little sea-dog led his fleet of twenty-four ships right into Cadiz harbour and destroyed more than a hundred Spanish vessels, as well as a vast quantity of stores. In this way he delayed the invasion for a whole year and gave his countrymen more time to prepare for it.

The Armada

Elizabeth roused the enthusiasm of her subjects to fever-heat by putting on armour and riding to Tilbury on a great war-horse to review the troops. 'I know I have but the body of a weak and feeble woman,' she said, 'but I have the heart of a king – and of a king of England, too!'

There is no room to tell here the story of the great encounter by which this island was saved. Proudly they set out, those floating castles which made up the Invincible Armada. One hundred and thirty there were, with 30,000 sailors and soldiers, and nearly 3000 cannon. Fifty-three of them, spent and broken, crept home nearly five months afterwards. All the rest, together with 20,000 men, had perished through the courage and better seamanship of the English, or in the gales that followed them all through that weary, panic-stricken flight.

The fear of that long-threatened invasion having passed away, England entered upon a kind of Golden Age. At last she was able to enjoy peace, and all the blessings which peace brings.

From *Newnes' Pictorial Knowledge*, a children's encyclopaedia written in the 1930s.

Enquiry Step 2: Suggesting an answer

Working in a small group, record on a table like this what *Newnes' Pictorial Knowledge* suggests about:	Whose fault the war was	
	Drake	
	Elizabeth	
	Why the Armada failed	
	What the results of the failure of the Armada were for England	

The myth of the Spanish Armada

You will have realised, I hope, that the story of the Armada in *Newnes' Pictorial Knowledge* was the old '**Whig** version of history'! The basic facts were true. Philip did send an Armada. It sailed up the Channel and harboured in Calais. There, the English sent in fireships which forced the Spanish to disperse, and there followed a six-day battle in the North Sea. The Spanish tried to make their way home round the north of Scotland, and their fleet was destroyed by storms.

But think about how *Newnes' Pictorial Knowledge* interpreted those facts:

- The cause of the war was ... Philip II, trying to conquer England and steal 'our' freedom.
- The Armada was defeated by ... English heroism – Drake's heroism, Elizabeth's inspiring speech, and the courageous seamanship of the English sailors.
- And the result was ... that England was saved from foreign invasion, and set on its destined journey to a great overseas empire.

For many English historians ever after, the Armada has been the moment when the Spanish were 'thrashed beyond redemption', and the time when the English 'saved their country and their liberty'. But how valid is that interpretation?

Read the fact boxes on page 131, and then answer the questions to decide how you would interpret the Armada.

Enquiry Step 3: Developing your answer

I Working in a small group, add a column to your table from page 129, and record there what the facts on pages 130–131 suggest about:

Whose fault the war was		
Drake		
Elizabeth		
Why the Armada failed		
What the results of the failure of the Armada were for England		

2 As a whole class, discuss how the facts challenge the Whig interpretation of the Armada.

C

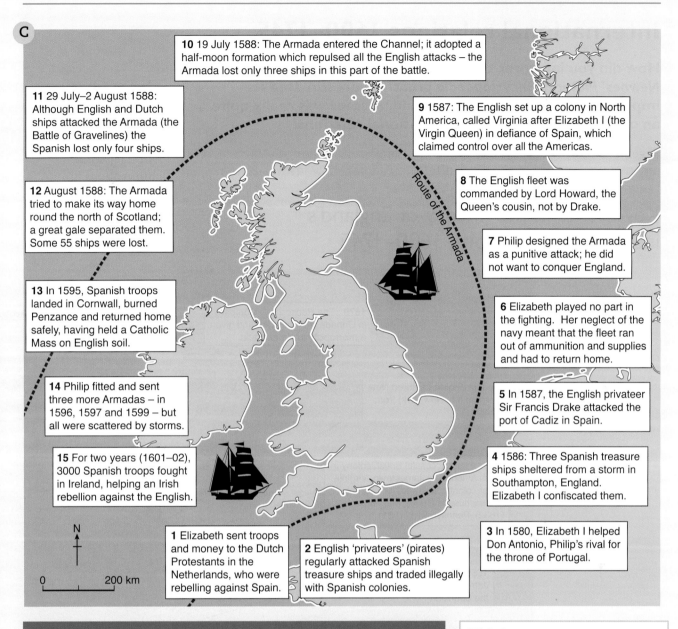

10 19 July 1588: The Armada entered the Channel; it adopted a half-moon formation which repulsed all the English attacks – the Armada lost only three ships in this part of the battle.

11 29 July–2 August 1588: Although English and Dutch ships attacked the Armada (the Battle of Gravelines) the Spanish lost only four ships.

12 August 1588: The Armada tried to make its way home round the north of Scotland; a great gale separated them. Some 55 ships were lost.

13 In 1595, Spanish troops landed in Cornwall, burned Penzance and returned home safely, having held a Catholic Mass on English soil.

14 Philip fitted and sent three more Armadas – in 1596, 1597 and 1599 – but all were scattered by storms.

15 For two years (1601–02), 3000 Spanish troops fought in Ireland, helping an Irish rebellion against the English.

9 1587: The English set up a colony in North America, called Virginia after Elizabeth I (the Virgin Queen) in defiance of Spain, which claimed control over all the Americas.

8 The English fleet was commanded by Lord Howard, the Queen's cousin, not by Drake.

7 Philip designed the Armada as a punitive attack; he did not want to conquer England.

6 Elizabeth played no part in the fighting. Her neglect of the navy meant that the fleet ran out of ammunition and supplies and had to return home.

5 In 1587, the English privateer Sir Francis Drake attacked the port of Cadiz in Spain.

4 1586: Three Spanish treasure ships sheltered from a storm in Southampton, England. Elizabeth I confiscated them.

3 In 1580, Elizabeth I helped Don Antonio, Philip's rival for the throne of Portugal.

Route of the Armada

N

0   200 km

1 Elizabeth sent troops and money to the Dutch Protestants in the Netherlands, who were rebelling against Spain.

2 English 'privateers' (pirates) regularly attacked Spanish treasure ships and traded illegally with Spanish colonies.

Enquiry Step 4: Concluding your enquiry

Write your own interpretation of the Armada under three headings:
  a) Causes   b) Why it Failed   c) Results
You will want to mention the Whig interpretation of the Armada, but make sure that you explain and support with facts YOUR version of events.

Think

How would you reply to someone who suggested that, 'In the sixteenth century, England was a rogue pirate nation'?

International relations 1600–1745

How did you interpret the Armada? Did you decide that
Newnes' Pictorial Encyclopaedia **greatly overestimated its importance, and that England in Tudor times was really quite an unimportant country in international relations?**

Pages 132–33 will allow you to judge whether Britain's foreign affairs were any more successful in the years after the Tudors – how far was Britain becoming a world superpower by 1745?

Key events in the history of England's international relations, 1600–1745

Think

Does the evidence on pages 132–133 support the assertion that 'English interventions in European wars tended to be unsuccessful'?

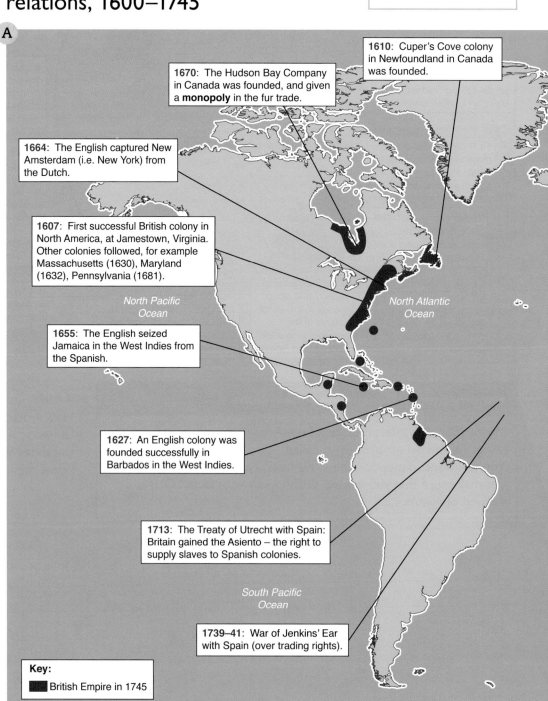

A

1610: Cuper's Cove colony in Newfoundland in Canada was founded.

1670: The Hudson Bay Company in Canada was founded, and given a **monopoly** in the fur trade.

1664: The English captured New Amsterdam (i.e. New York) from the Dutch.

1607: First successful British colony in North America, at Jamestown, Virginia. Other colonies followed, for example Massachusetts (1630), Maryland (1632), Pennsylvania (1681).

North Pacific Ocean

North Atlantic Ocean

1655: The English seized Jamaica in the West Indies from the Spanish.

1627: An English colony was founded successfully in Barbados in the West Indies.

1713: The Treaty of Utrecht with Spain: Britain gained the Asiento – the right to supply slaves to Spanish colonies.

South Pacific Ocean

1739–41: War of Jenkins' Ear with Spain (over trading rights).

Key:
■ British Empire in 1745

132

Activity

1 Working in a small group, sort the events in map A into three categories:
▌ European Wars
▌ Trade and Empire
▌ Diplomacy and Alliances.
What do you notice?

2 Judging from the eighteen events described on pages 132–133, would you say that Britain had become a world superpower by 1745? If not, what would you say?

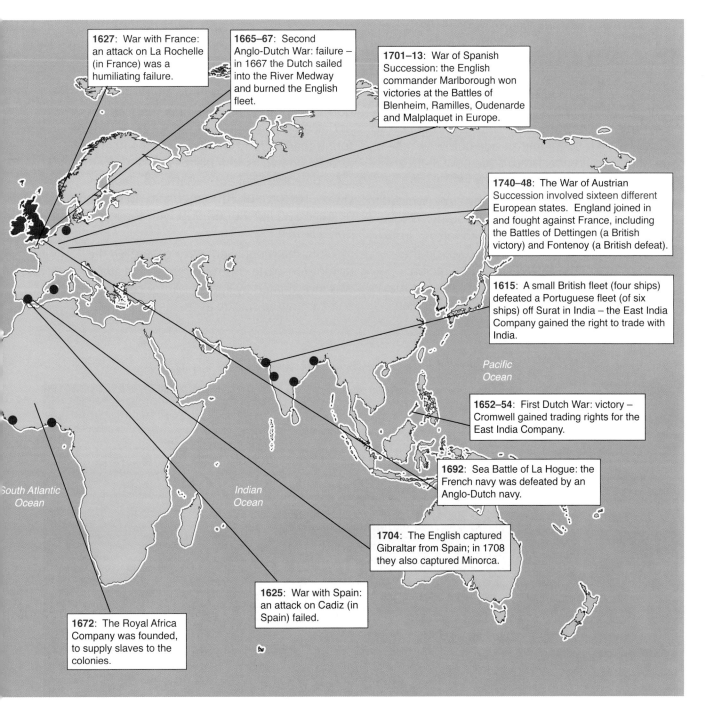

1627: War with France: an attack on La Rochelle (in France) was a humiliating failure.

1665–67: Second Anglo-Dutch War: failure – in 1667 the Dutch sailed into the River Medway and burned the English fleet.

1701–13: War of Spanish Succession: the English commander Marlborough won victories at the Battles of Blenheim, Ramilles, Oudenarde and Malplaquet in Europe.

1740–48: The War of Austrian Succession involved sixteen different European states. England joined in and fought against France, including the Battles of Dettingen (a British victory) and Fontenoy (a British defeat).

1615: A small British fleet (four ships) defeated a Portuguese fleet (of six ships) off Surat in India – the East India Company gained the right to trade with India.

Pacific Ocean

1652–54: First Dutch War: victory – Cromwell gained trading rights for the East India Company.

1692: Sea Battle of La Hogue: the French navy was defeated by an Anglo-Dutch navy.

South Atlantic Ocean

Indian Ocean

1704: The English captured Gibraltar from Spain; in 1708 they also captured Minorca.

1625: War with Spain: an attack on Cadiz (in Spain) failed.

1672: The Royal Africa Company was founded, to supply slaves to the colonies.

Why did the British Empire grow in the eighteenth century?

On pages 132–133 you saw how the British Empire began to grow in the seventeenth and eighteenth centuries. Now it is time to investigate why.

It was a question which teachers never addressed in the 1960s. What schoolchildren learned then, instead, were the stories of the 'great people' – as one writer called them – who built the Empire. They were stories of high adventure, told in an exciting way. It taught that the Empire grew because of the achievements of individuals, whom pupils were encouraged to copy.

Let's start with summaries of two of the stories:

A

The story of Robert Clive

Robert Clive was a wild boy and a dunce at school, and his father sent him to be a clerk in the **East India Company**, largely to get rid of him. There he tried to commit suicide but, when the gun failed to fire, declared: 'I see now that I am meant to make something of my life!'

He joined the East India Company army, which at the time was being driven out of southern India by an alliance of French and Indian forces. In 1751, Clive proposed a counter-attack on the town of Arcot, the capital city of the region. Given a force of just 500 men, he captured the town and held it for 53 days against an Indian army of 4000 trying to retake it.

Five years later, another Indian ruler, Siraj-ud-doulah, captured the East India Company base at Calcutta, and imprisoned the 146 Britons he found there (123 of them died in the heat – an atrocity known as 'the Black Hole of Calcutta'). Clive defeated Siraj at the Battle of Plassey (1757), his force of 3000 men and 40 cannons defeating an army of 68,000 with the loss of only 23 men.

In 1765, the Mughal emperor gave Clive the diwany (absolute control) of Bengal. Later, Clive was investigated by Parliament for corruption, and committed suicide at the age of 49.

⬇ 'Clive himself sprang to a gun', from *The Romance of Empire – India* (1909) by Victor Surridge.

B

C

← A printed engraving (c.1870) of James Wolfe dying heroically at Quebec, by the English artist Edward Corbould.

D

The story of James Wolfe

James Wolfe was the son of a soldier. He was a sickly child, but he made up in courage what he lacked in strength. At the age of 13, he joined the **Marines**. By the age of 21 he had fought in seven campaigns; by the age of 31 he was a general. He was a tough commander – desertion was punished with the death penalty.

In 1759 he was given the task of capturing Quebec in Canada from the brilliant French commander Montcalm. After a fruitless siege of three months, and seriously ill (probably with tuberculosis), Wolfe led a desperate surprise night-manoeuvre up the cliffs behind the town, which were thought to be unclimbable. The next morning, the French awoke to an army and two cannons at the gates, and were defeated in a 15-minute battle.

Wolfe, however, was killed in the fight – his dying words were to give orders to cut off the French retreat. As a result of his bravery and sacrifice, soon the whole of Canada was added to the British Empire.

The causes of the growth of the British Empire

Before the 1970s, teachers rarely addressed the question of why the British gained an empire in the seventeenth and eighteenth centuries because, in a sense, they didn't need to. The answer in those days was taken as read – the triumph of Parliament and Protestantism in 1688, along with the superior British character, made the Empire inevitable! Empire, children were taught, was Britain's destiny. Nowadays, however, it is a question that historians believe they need to consider. Here are seven different causes, in no particular order:

1 Technology

Before the eighteenth century, although sailors could measure **latitude**, they could not measure **longitude**. Ships therefore could not know exactly where they were and were often wrecked when they literally bumped into land they thought was miles away. From the 1730s sea-travel became much safer, as a result of the availability of better steel (a result of the **Industrial Revolution**), and the invention of reliable sea-clocks which improved navigation.

2 The Industrial Revolution

The British economy grew steadily from 1688. The Industrial Revolution stimulated trade, and increased Britain's wealth ... and, in wars, victory usually goes to the wealthiest.

3 The Navy

After its victory in the battle of La Hogue (1692), the British Navy was probably the most powerful navy on earth. It grew even more powerful in the years up to 1745. It developed better 'fighting instructions' (based on **'ships-of-the-line'** making a co-ordinated attack). It captured naval bases around the world (for example, Gibraltar) where its ships could restock and refit. And it developed the 'frigate' – a smaller ship with at least 28 guns used to protect British traders.

4 The Slave Trade

The slave trade was a crime against humanity, but it generated huge wealth in the ports (like Bristol and Liverpool) from which the slave traders sailed ... and this wealth then helped to grow the British economy. It also provided the workers with which the British developed their empire in the West Indies and North America.

5 Navigation acts

In 1651, the government passed the first of the **Navigation Acts**, which stated that trade with British colonies could only be carried in British ships. This meant that all the profits of Britain's overseas trade flowed into the British economy, and this gave the money and the incentive to traders to go out and establish more colonies and trading posts.

6 Trade

The government did not conquer the overseas empire. Instead, it gave 'charters' to trading companies (such as the East India Company). It was these companies which established the trading posts, factories, forts and colonies – and fought and defeated rival traders – as part of that trade, which grew increasingly rapidly after 1688.

7 France's wars

If you look at map C on page 127 you will see that at the end of the seventeenth century both the French (in blue) and the Dutch (in orange) also had large overseas empires. However, in the eighteenth century, both France and Holland were distracted and eventually ruined by a series of wars in Europe. This gave an opportunity to British traders to expand overseas.

Activity

1 Working in a small group, discuss each cause in turn. Explain HOW it might have worked to help the British Empire to grow.

2 The spider diagram on the right shows the seven factors which caused the British Empire to grow. In your group, draw lines between the factors where you can show there was a link. What do you notice?

3 After your work on Clive and Wolfe on pages 134–135, do you want to add 'Individual achievement' as an eighth cause?

4 Working as a whole class, discuss the question:

Why did the British Empire grow in the years before 1745?

Put the seven causes (or eight if you added 'individual achievement') into rank order of importance. What criteria did you use to decide?

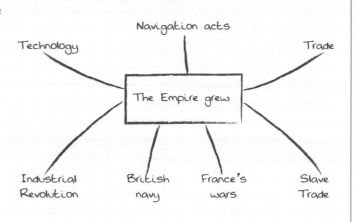

So did Britannia 'rule the waves' in 1745?

You started off this section by looking at the Armada. Even if you didn't go the whole way and declare the Armada a non-event – you must have realised that Elizabeth's 'glorious victory' was not as great as it has been portrayed! It could be argued that during Tudor times, Britain was a small, pirate 'rogue nation' and only the weather (and the help of the Dutch) saved it from its comeuppance.

On the other hand, in the chapter: 'International relations, 1600–1745'– although England's interventions in European wars tended to be unsuccessful – you saw that England began to acquire an overseas empire. Then, in the chapter 'Why did the British Empire grow in the eighteenth century?', you learned that the Empire's growth was based on the huge wealth generated by Britain's industrial and trade revolutions (and the fact that the two other maritime empires of France and Holland were fighting each other to the death in Europe).

Do you believe that this made England 'a world power' by 1745? Personally – compared to the real empires of the time, such as the Mughals in India and the Ming dynasty in China – my feeling would be that some coastal settlements in North America, a few Caribbean islands and a scattering of trading posts in Africa and India did NOT make England 'a world power' in 1745, especially as the year saw a dangerous rebellion (the '45 see page 124) and a huge military defeat (at Fontenoy).

Yet, every year, at the 'Last Night of the Proms' at the Royal Albert Hall in London, tens of thousands of British people sing, at the top of their voices, verses from a song first performed in 1745:

A

Rule Britannia!

When Britain first, at heaven's command,
Arose from out the azure main,
Arose, arose, arose from out the azure main,
This was the charter, the charter of the land,
And guardian angels sang this strain:

Rule Britannia! Britannia rule the waves.
Britons never, never, never shall be slaves.

The nations, not so blest as thee,
Must in their turn, to tyrants fall,
While thou shalt flourish, shalt flourish great and free,
The dread and envy of them all.

Still more majestic shalt thou rise,
More dreadful from each foreign stroke,
As the loud blast that tears the skies
Serves but to root thy native oak.

The Muses, still with freedom found,
Shall to thy happy coasts repair.
Blest isle! with matchless beauty crowned,
And manly hearts to guard the fair.

The 'azure main': 'azure' is blue, and the 'Spanish Main' was the Caribbean Sea where English pirates plundered Spanish treasure-ships in the sixteenth century.

Native oak: a symbol of freedom, wisdom, and permanence. Incidentally, also, the ships of the British Navy were made from oak.

The Muses were Greek goddesses who symbolised the different arts and sciences.

B

⬆ For the 2009 'Last Night', Sarah Connolly sang *Rule Britannia* dressed as a nineteenth-century Admiral. Huge crowds waved Union flags and joined in the chorus. 'As a party the Last Night is pretty good', commented *The Telegraph* newspaper. 'As a piece of cultural/political manipulation, it's a masterpiece.'

Activity

1 You can see, in the song *Rule Britannia*, the historical beginnings of the Whig interpretation of history! Working with a partner or in a small group, find where in the song the words exemplify the 'Whig' ideas that:
   ▌ the British were better than other nations
   ▌ British foreign policy was about political freedom
   ▌ British freedoms dated back to Magna Carta
   ▌ British freedoms brought learning and culture in their wake
   ▌ you can see the 'seeds' of the British Empire in Elizabethan times
   ▌ the rise of Britain to world power status was unstoppable
   ▌ the rise of Britain was divinely ordained – destined by God
   ▌ history is essentially 'male'.

2 The areas coloured red on map C on page 127 show the extent of England's colonial empire and trading posts in 1745. Coming together as a whole class, discuss:

   Did Britain 'rule the waves' in 1745?

Think

Referring to picture B, explain how the song *Rule Britannia* (and the Whig interpretation of history) is 'cultural/ political manipulation'.

A peep into the future – the difference twenty years can make!

Officially, this book ends our period of study at 1745. However, in this final chapter, we will take a peep forward at the Seven Years' War, 1756–63. The end date you choose significantly affects the conclusion you come to for the question: Did Britannia rule the waves?

The War of Austrian Succession (1740–48) – which you encountered on page 133 – had started when the German state of Prussia invaded Austria. The Treaty of Aix-la-Chapelle which ended it solved nothing because it merely restored everything to what it had been before the war. So it was no great surprise when fighting broke out again.

The Seven Years' War started when Prussia invaded the German state of Saxony, but before long fifteen countries were involved in the fighting. Britain, again, joined in to fight against the French.

Opening defeats

The Seven Years' War was the first 'world' war, with fighting all over the world.

For the British, at first, it looked as though the war was going to be a disaster. They suffered a string of defeats in North America. They lost the naval base of Minorca. The British army in Europe was defeated at the Battle of Hastenbeck. And, in India, a French force captured Madras town, and by December 1758 had opened a breach in the walls of the British fort there.

Things were going so badly that, in 1759, people in Britain were preparing for a French invasion.

Annus Mirabilis

But then, in 1759, everything changed. It was a 'year of miracles' (*Annus Mirabilis*) which changed the course of history.

By the Treaty of Paris which ended the war (1763), Britain gained total control of North America and dominated India. Minorca was returned, and – although the British gave up Guadeloupe – the French handed over the sugar islands of Tobago, St Vincent and Dominica in the West Indies.

Soon after, the British statesman George Macartney coined the description of the British empire as one 'on which the sun never sets', adding: 'and whose boundaries nature has not yet fixed'.

 A

Annus Mirabilis

The modern historian Frank McLynn calls 1759: 'The year Britain became master of the world':

- Britain paid £670,000 (equivalent to £10 billion today) a year to its ally, Frederick II of Prussia; he kept France's allies Russia and Austria busy in eastern Europe.
- To prevent a French invasion, the British navy blockaded the French navy in the ports at Toulon and Brest.
- In February, a fleet of six British ships, with 600 troops, arrived at Madras and relieved the garrison; French influence in India collapsed.
- In May, a British force of naval marines captured the West Indian sugar island of Guadeloupe from the French.
- In August, a British army of 37,000 defeated a French army of 40,000 after the British infantry mistook their orders and attacked – and, to everyone's amazement, put to flight – the French cavalry.
- In August, the French fleet at Toulon sailed out; it was defeated at the Battle of Lagos.
- In September, Wolfe took Quebec (see page 135), and with it control of the whole of North America.
- In November, the French fleet at Brest sailed out; it was defeated at the Battle of Quiberon Bay.

B

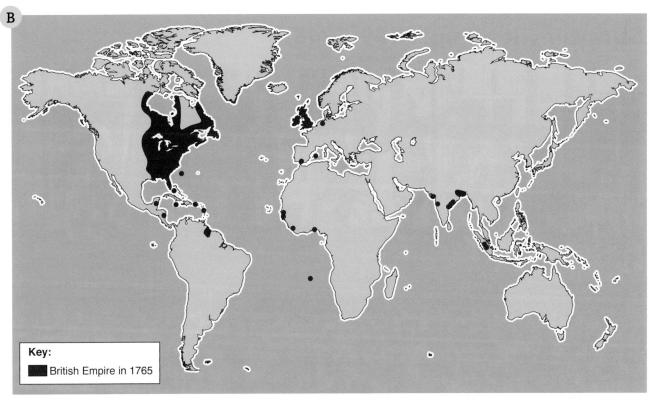

⬆ The British Empire in 1765. The British Navy was indisputably the most powerful fleet in the world.

Activity

1 Working in a small group, analyse the eight 'surprise' victories in extract A on page 140 against the seven factors which caused the British Empire to grow in the spider diagram on the right.

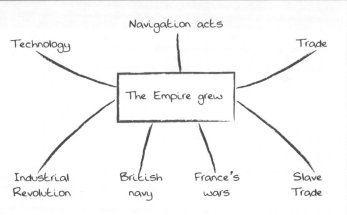

For each of the victories, identify the causes that played a part in that victory.
▌ Which was the most important cause?
▌ Which was the most surprising victory?

2 In 1992, Denmark won the Euro '92 football competition when they had actually failed to qualify, and had only got into the competition because Yugoslavia was disqualified; the victory was a complete 'bombshell' surprise. By contrast, Andy Murray's Wimbledon victory in 2013 was not such a surprise, when you consider how many years he had trained, how well he was playing, and the fact that he had recently won the Olympic gold medal – there was a good chance that he would win the title eventually.

Given your answers to question 1, was the *Annus Mirabilis* a Denmark-style bombshell, or a Murray-like inevitability?

3 Coming together as a whole class, discuss this idea:

'The conclusion about whether Britannia ruled the waves depends on the end date you choose – the answer in 1745 is "No", but the answer in 1765 is "Yes"?'

Summing it all up, 1509–1745

**A main aim of all the books in this series is the same –
to leave you with 'a sense of period'.**

Developing a 'sense of period' involves more than simply learning
a few dates and facts – it means developing an empathy (a 'feel')
for the people and their lives ... understanding WHY the age was
like it was.

The History National Curriculum for Key Stage 3 divides British
History up into four periods – Medieval (1066–1509), Early Modern
Era (1509–1745), the Industrial Revolution (1745–1901) and Modern
(1901 to the present day). Each era is distinctive and different
from the others, with different technologies, different political
ideas, and different attitudes and beliefs. How have we done in
this book for leaving you with a 'sense of period'? Do you feel you
understand what the Early Modern Era was about?

In Book 1 – if you used it to study the Middle Ages – we finished by
telling you about the period. In this book we are going to let you
develop your own interpretation. This section will help you
organise your ideas.

Working in a small group, do the following:

1 We started the book (pages 2–3) with a picture of what we called the 'defining event of the period' – the execution of Charles I in 1649. Then we spent Section 6 asking you to study its significance.

   The 'defining event of the period' is going to be the event which best sums up what the period was about – would you have chosen 1649? If not, suggest some other events which, for you, better illustrate the age. Use some of the pictures throughout the book to help you.

2 Looking back through the book, choose what you think are the most important events of the era. Justify your choices. Share your ideas with other groups, and use their ideas to refine and change your own list.

3 Two large-scale occurrences underlie much of what happened in Early Modern Britain:

   ▌ Rising prices (see pages 20–21, 28, 34 and 64)
   ▌ The 'Little Ice Age' (and the failed harvests, epidemics and storms it caused – see pages 6–7, 20–21, 31, 117, 121 and 131.

   What did these two developments affect … and how? Are there any other developments or ideas which you think underlie the entire age?

4 We divided up your studies into different aspects – 'People's Lives' (Section 3), 'Beliefs' (Section 4), 'Power' (Section 6), 'Making the United Kingdom' (Section 8), and 'Warfare and empire' (Section 9).

   ▌ Look back and review your learning in each of these sections. Each one will have helped to create your 'sense of period', but which aspect most dominates your impression of the times?
   ▌ Rank them in terms of how important each was in contributing to your 'sense of period'.

5 You also studied Mughal India, 1626–1707 (Section 7). Mr Kennett, the author of that section, drew parallels between Mughal India and Britain at the time.

   ▌ Look back at Section 7. How different do you think Mughal India was to Tudor and Stuart Britain?
   ▌ Explain how studying those differences helped your developing 'sense of period' about Early Modern Britain.

6 On page 11, we introduced you to the Whig interpretation of history – that, in this period, Britain gradually, unstoppably and inevitably progressed towards the wealth, democracy and empire, which was her national destiny.

   Do you agree? As a historian, what is your interpretation of Britain's history in the years 1509–1745?

7 Choose the 'most interesting topics' you have learned about. Justify your choices.

'A sense of period'

The entries in the tables on these pages are just our suggestions, of course!
You will have your own opinions about the Middle Ages, and you will be
forming your opinion of later times in Books 3 and 4 of this series.

	Middle Ages, 1066–1509	Early Modern Era, 1509–1745
1	Norman Conquest, Magna Carta, Black Death	Activity 1a
2	William I, Edward I, Edward III	Activity 1b
3	Peasants' Revolt	Activity 1c
4	Murder of Thomas Becket	Activity 1d
5	Royal rulers, rebellions and the beginning of Parliament	Activity 1e
6	A time of disease and warfare	Activity 1f

Activity

1 Debate and take a class vote to choose:
   a) the THREE 'most important events of the period'
   b) the THREE 'most important people of the period'
   c) the most interesting topic
   d) the 'defining event'
   e) the most important issue(s) in government.
   f) Finally, choose TWO or THREE words which, for you, together sum up
      the period 1509–1745; make them into a sentence which starts with the
      words: 'A time of ...' and which 'sums up the age'. Share your sentence
      with other groups, and use their comments and ideas to refine your
      own sentence.

Industrial Age, 1745–1901	Modern Age, 1901–present
Industrial Revolution, French Revolution, Ireland	1930s Depression, Holocaust, Welfare State
I.K. Brunel, Charles Darwin, Lord Shaftesbury	Hitler, Stalin, Churchill
The abolition of the slave trade	Life behind the Iron Curtain
The early industrialists	First World War
The coming of democracy	Fascism and communism
A time of technological and medical advance	A time of mass-consumption, overshadowed by the threat of nuclear warfare

Activity

2 Finally, write 250 words on:

Britain in the Early Modern Era, 1509–1745.

Start with the rhetorical question: How do we define 'the Early Modern Era in Britain?' then write sentences on:

▌ The three most important events, the three most important people, and the most interesting topic of the period.

▌ The defining event of the period, and how it 'sums up the age'.

▌ The most important issue(s) in government.

▌ How the Whigs interpreted, and how you interpret, the events of the period.

▌ Finish with your summative sentence from question 1f.

Glossary

Absolutism The belief that a monarch should have total ('absolute') power to do anything they wished, without the restraint of Parliament.

Altar The stone table at the east end of a church where the service of the Mass is performed.

Aristocracy People who hold a title – lords, baronets, etc.

Biased Not impartial; favouring one side over the other.

Black Death One of the most devastating epidemics of infectious disease resulting in the deaths of an estimated 75 to 200 million people and peaking in Europe in the years 1348–50.

Black market The underground economy or market in which goods or services are traded illegally.

Bubonic plague An infectious disease which is believed to be the cause of the Black Death that swept through Europe in the fourteenth century. There were regular outbreaks of bubonic plague every ten years or so; the last – the Great Plague of London in 1665 – killed up to 200,000 people.

Carding Brushing the raw wool to align the strands prior to spinning.

Civil War A war between opposing factions within a country – in this context, the wars between king and Parliament, 1642–49.

Court The group of people usually around the monarch – primarily their ministers and leading nobles.

Courtiers The people close to the monarch – their friends, favourites and leading nobles.

Communists People who follow the political and economic teachings of the nineteenth century writer Karl Marx (hence, sometimes, 'Marxists').

Coronation Oath The promises made by the monarch when they are crowned.

Cottagers Poorer people, who lived in small rural cottages.

Deity Another word for 'God'.

Disembowel Cut open and remove a person's internal organs. It was cruel because it was not immediately fatal.

Divine Right The theory that, because the monarch was appointed by God, they could do whatever they wished, and the people had a religious duty to obey.

East India Company An English company, which received its royal charter in 1600. It was set up to trade with India and the Far East. From 1757 until 1858 it ruled India.

Economist A person who understands how the economy – the world of business, trade and finance – works.

Enclosure The process by which Common Land was taken from the community and shared between local landowners; it was so-called because they built a fence to 'enclose' their newly-acquired land.

Excommunicate To be expelled from the Roman Catholic Church and therefore be unable to get to Heaven.

Fraternity The belief that all men are 'brothers'.

Garter King of Arms The senior officer of the College of Arms which records the pedigree and coats of arms of Britain's noble families. Thomas Wriothesley held the title from 1505 to 1534 (under Henry VIII).

Gentry People of high social class, though not aristocrats – e.g. lords of the manor, knights, rich landowners, etc.

Heresy Beliefs not allowed by the Church or the monarch

His Majesty's Opposition The minority party/parties in Parliament, which have the right and the duty to oppose the government.

House arrest Imprisonment in one's own house (rather than in prison or the Tower of London).

Hurdle A wooden rectangular frame.

Illiterate Unable to read or write.

Indoctrinated Brainwashed.

Indulgences Papers, given by the Roman Catholic Church upon payment of a sum of money, which guaranteed the forgiveness of sins and a fast track into Heaven.

Industrial Revolution The expansion of the British economy after 1750.

Interregnum The period between (Latin: *inter*) reigns (Latin: *regnum*); in our context, the period between the execution of Charles I in 1649 and the restoration of Charles II in 1660.

Jacobite A person who supported the right of James II and his successors to the throne of England; from the Latin word for James (*Jacobus*).

Justice of the Peace A local magistrate appointed to keep the peace, hear minor legal cases, and ensure that the Poor Laws were being maintained.

Latitude The lines which go east to west on a map of the earth.

Longitude The lines which go from the North to the South Pole on a map of the Earth.

Lord Protector The title used by Oliver Cromwell because he did not want to call himself 'king'.

Marines Soldiers who fight from a ship – e.g. in amphibious landings.

Marxist People who follow the political and economic teachings of the nineteenth century writer Karl Marx (i.e., 'Communists').

Mass The name given by the Roman Catholic Church to the service at which the bread and wine are given (in the Church of England, 'Communion' or 'Eucharist').

Monopoly Where the monarch gave their favourites the sole right to trade in a commodity (allowing them to make huge profits).

Navigation Acts Laws passed by the English Parliament that all goods traded to or from England or the colonies had to be carried in English ships.

Nave The main body of the church, excluding the altar and the choir.

Nimrod A person in the Bible; in our context, a man who lived thousands of years ago.

Out-relief Payments to poor people in their own homes; poor relief which did not require them to enter the workhouse.

Papal ambassador The representative of the Pope in a foreign country.

Parliamentarian A supporter of Parliament during the Civil Wars.

Pastor A church minister or priest.

Persians People from the area around modern-day Iran.

Petition of Right Parliament's demand, in 1629, that Charles promise not to imprison people without trial, or take forced loans.

Pillory A kind of stocks, where the victim stood.

Pious Godly, and religiously-minded.

Population ceiling Where the growth in population is limited by the amount of food available.

Quakers A religious sect which believes in quiet meditation and a personal experience of God.

Radical Extreme, revolutionary, wanting great change.

Rates Money paid by landowners to the Parish Council – council tax.

Reformation A period of violent change in religion, especially in northern Europe, when 'Protestant' Christians rejected the Roman Catholic Church.

Refute To argue (successfully) against a person or idea.

Rood Screen The wooden screen in an old church which separates the nave from the choir.

Royalist Someone who supported the king during the Civil Wars.

Salon A social and intellectual gathering, usually in the house of a famous lady, where people talked about politics and culture.

Satirist A writer who uses sarcasm or ridicule to make a point about society or politics.

Sermon A religious message, usually delivered in church.

Shari'ah law The legal code of the Islamic faith.

Ships-of-the-line Ships of the Royal Navy, so called because they attacked in a line.

Slave trade The practice of taking Africans to sell as slaves in America and the West Indies.

The Spanish Main The areas of mainland America (Florida, Mexico and the north coast of South America) which surrounded the Caribbean Sea (as opposed to the islands of the Caribbean (the West Indies).

Standard of living Quality of life, especially as determined by one's money income.

Statistician Someone skilled in the analysis of statistics.

Succession Passing on the crown to an heir.

Sweating sickness An unknown (probably viral) epidemic fever common in the Early Modern Era.

Swivel gun A small cannon, mounted on a swivelling stand or fork which allows a very wide arc of movement. They were principally used aboard sailing ships.

Transportation As a punishment short of hanging, convicted criminals and rebels might be sent to the colonies, especially Australia and New Zealand.

The Tower The Tower of London, where traitors were imprisoned and executed.

Vestments The clothes worn by Church clergy.

Villeins A villager who was not free and had to work on the lord's land for a number of days every week without pay.

War elephants Elephants used in warfare. Their main use was to charge the enemy, trampling them and breaking their ranks and instilling terror. They were first employed in India, the practice spreading out across south-east Asia and westwards into the Mediterranean.

Whigs A political party which grew up in the 1680s to oppose Catholicism, absolutism and the 'Tories' who supported the king. The term 'Whig historian' dates from the 1920s, and describes an historian who believes that England's greatness came inevitably from the Whig opposition to the king.

Workhouse A place where poor people were sent to receive poor relief.

Index